WHO'S IN YOUR ROOM?

THE QUALITY OF YOUR LIFE DEPENDS ON THE PEOPLE IN YOUR LIFE

Stewart Emery

Ivan Misner

Rick Sapio

BNI Edition

A Paradigm Publishing Book

Paradigm Publishing titles may be purchased in bulk for educational, business, fund-raising, or sales promotional use. For information, please e-mail misner@bni.com

ISBN: 978-0-615-97591-7

Printed in the United States of America

To all the people
in our rooms.

Table of Contents

Foward
By Ivan Misner

Some time ago, I was pleased to sit through a presentation by Stewart Emery at a Transformational Leadership Council meeting. I always love hearing Stewart talk. However, on this particular occasion, what he had to say hit me right between the eyes.

He advanced an interesting series of questions and ideas to the audience. He asked us: *"What if you had to live your life in one room? Everyone you want to interact with in life is in that room. There is only one door, and that door works only one way. Whoever is in your room stays in your room forever, and impacts your life directly in many ways. If you knew that a certain person would be in your room forever, would you have let that individual into your room?"*

He went on to ask, *"If you decided to let everyone in, what would your room be like? Would it be an angry room, a chaotic room, a happy room, a conflicted room or a peaceful room? Would there be a lot of drama with too many people present and too many interruptions?"*

Stewart's point was that the quality of your life and your business is a direct reflection of who is in your room. How you manage who you let into your room (and your life) is very important. How do we go about choosing who we let in? He suggested that we employ a virtual "doorman," someone who knows your values and your passions. The doorman can keep people from getting into your life who conflict with your values, who would prevent you from becoming the person you want to be.

He then asked us to do an exercise, to think about the people who are in our room right now. Are there people close to us (in our room) who don't live up to our values? Would we have let them in if we had thought about this concept before allowing them to get close to us?

We design and decorate the room we live in, along with choosing the people we let into it. We can do this consciously or we can do it mindlessly, by happenstance. The choice is ours. The question now becomes: who are we going to let into our room from this point forward?

When Stewart was finished with his presentation, I realized that what he had just described was the perfect metaphor for a chapter of BNI! Chapters can be successful or can totally fail directly as a result of who they let into their room. If the chapter is a positive, supportive, productive group, it is because members have let in positive, supportive, productive individuals. If it is a lackluster, uncommitted, or unhappy group, it is because they've generally let in members who are lackluster, uncommitted, or unhappy.

For BNI, this is more than a metaphor—it is our reality. Who we let into a group determines how successful the group ultimately becomes. Even more fitting, we actually have a "doorman"! The BNI doorman is the Membership Committee of every group, which is the keeper of the values and commitments of a chapter. The committee, along with the other members, determines who is in our room. The membership committee, in many ways, is the most important element of a long-term successful group.

The people we allow to become close to us should be people we want to work with. They should be people who share our values and our passions. Understanding this simple concept (and applying it) can help us to comprehend the difference between an opportunity and a distraction. It can help us choose between an individual who we think has a skill set we need versus someone who has both the skill set and a value set we wish to bring to life.

Who's in Your Room? is a book that is incredibly relevant to BNI. Our program is not only a great way to "get" business; it is an even better way to "do" business. In order to make this a reality, we have to bring people into our room who we truly look forward to doing business with.

Introduction

Alex Mandossian was late. It was not normally like him to be late, although (mostly in jest) he would periodically complain that I am chronically on time.

Alex was a little over 15 minutes late for our meeting when he hurried through the door, into the meeting room and offered apologies. He said, by way of explanation, that on the drive down he had received a call from his friend, Rick Sapio. One of Rick's core passions in life is championing the entrepreneurial spirit, something he believes lives in many more people than actually become entrepreneurs. He holds that the core trait of successful entrepreneurs is being accountable for outcomes. Rick believes that any of us can develop this trait and become successful entrepreneurs, and successful in all aspects of life.

Rick was calling to invite Alex to an entrepreneurial mastermind group on Richard Branson's Necker Island. Alex responded with a litany of reasons why he couldn't attend the gathering. Rick interrupted Alex and said, "We need to talk, and not while you're driving. Pull over someplace, so I can have your full attention." Alex did.

Rick then said, "Alex, you need a doorman."

"What do you mean I need a doorman? I don't live in a mansion. Why do I need a doorman?"

"Trust me you need a doorman. You've got too much going on in your life. You're addicted to saying 'Yes,' and you need a doorman to keep people and projects out of your room."

"And what room would that be?" asked Alex. The answer to this, and the question that follows it, have served as the catalyst for an ongoing dialogue between Rick, Ivan, me and hundreds of other people over the last several years, a dialogue that has developed into this book.

The subsequent question is this: "Who's in your room?"

It's a simple enough question on the face of it, but one that has had a profound effect on the lives of those who have tried to answer it, especially your authors. It's an idea that can be shared in a single sentence, yet has many diverse and even complex sides to it —what Hollywood would call "high concept."

Don't take our word for it, though. Explore the stories of those who have changed their lives for the better as a result of answering the question, and putting a doorman in place. The stories may not all resonate with you, but that's actually partly the point: we're all quite different, with different needs, yet each of us is likely to find several stories in this book that seem like they were tailored just for us.

In some of the stories you will find the actual names of people who discuss obstacles in their lives and how they overcame them. In other cases, out of regard for personal courtesy or privacy, full names aren't divulged. But they are all true stories from real people, with real outcomes and lessons.

Open the pages of this book and explore. And keep in mind, the exploration and discovery is not about the people whose stories are included here. It is about you!

Stewart Emery

Chapter 1
Imagine You Live in This Room

Imagine that you live in just one room. Imagine that you spend your entire life in this one room, a place where your imagination creates your world. This space includes all the people in your life, as well as the projects, relationships, and obligations that come along with them. It also contains all your own ambitions and dreams. You can continually update your room to include any and all new possibilities that you might like in your life.

There is one unique feature of this room that will never change—it has one door, and this door only operates one way: in. There is no exit; whoever comes through this door, and whatever they bring with them, cannot leave—ever. They will remain in your room—with you forever.

This is important because the quality of your life depends upon who's in your room.

> *Let me repeat that: The quality of your life depends upon who's in your room.*

This is one of those "good news/bad news" situations. Let's say your life is chaotic. Ask yourself: who are the people you let into your room who brought the chaos with them? Or maybe your life is harsh and angry. Who are the harsh and angry people in your room? Perhaps, on the other hand, your life is blessed with love and kindness. Who are those kind and loving people you invited into your room? If you are overwhelmed by complexity, then you probably have an overcrowded room. Do you want to be successful? Then you're going to need successful people in your room.

I think you get the idea. This concept is extraordinarily powerful. By having a sense of vigilance, and consciously choosing who is let into your room and who isn't, you will develop tremendous power to create the life you want for yourself, and become truly outstanding at anything you set your mind to. The phrase "transform your life" is highly overused, but that is exactly what we're talking about here.

When first introduced to this concept, many people experience an *OMG!* moment. Some launch into flashback mode, later saying that it was like watching a high-speed replay of their entire lives. A train wreck for some, just a bumpy ride for others.

Allow yourself to press pause. Stop for a moment and think. Who's in your room? Take a quick inventory. Ask yourself how you might have lived your life differently had you known that anybody you let into your room was going to be there forever. Then think about how, going forward, you are going to determine which people to let into your room, now that you know they can never leave?

Perhaps you have doubts. Maybe you are thinking, "It can't literally be true that once people get into my room, they are there forever." Consider it this way, then: Ask yourself if you would be willing, from this moment on, to live as though it were true. Neuroscientists have confirmed that this concept is actually true as far as your brain is concerned. Any input that is received into the "room" of your life triggers actual neural activity in your brain, generating information that cannot simply be erased or deleted as though it never happened.

For example, you might believe that you have ended a relationship, terminated a project, or let a previous commitment go. But those events have had an indelible impact. They will affect all your future experiences in myriad ways, whether you like it or not.

———

Some of you may have had grade school teachers who believed that people's IQ scores tell the whole story of who they are, and ranked the classroom in IQ order—who only trusted the highest IQ students to carry the flag, collect the homework or take a note to the principal. Or maybe you had a teacher who promoted a mindset in the class that it was essential to always appear smart, and never look dumb. If so, odds are good that you developed an obsession with proving yourself in life, whether it was in the classroom, in your career or in relationships. In every situation, you strive to prove that you are not dumb—that you are actually quite smart. Because of this, you feel you can never risk making a mistake or being wrong.

Perhaps, on the other hand, you were blessed with teachers who promoted the fundamental belief that people's essential qualities are things that can be cultivated through their own efforts. These kinds of teachers approach education from the point of view that although people may vary greatly in terms of talents and abilities, anyone can change and grow through learning and experience. Educators with this mindset believe that a young person's future is not foretold at the moment of their conception, and that it is impossible to predict what a person can accomplish when factors such as passion and concerted effort are brought to bear.

If you were blessed with teachers like these, then chances are good that you grew up with the belief that valued qualities can be developed—that talent is made and not born. As a result, your life today is likely full of passion for learning. These same kinds of teachers would also probably tell you that if you want to make your own talent, you had better be very discerning about who you let in your room.

———————————

The view you have of yourself, and whether you truly believe that you can develop into the person you want to be, profoundly affects the way you live your life. And the people in your room profoundly affect the view you have of yourself. In this very real way, your grade school teachers still live with you in your room, and continue to impact the quality of your life. Everyone in your room has a similar impact—whether it's a past love, a bully in school or the office, an in-law, a business partner, etc. Your room can get pretty crowded!

At this point, it doesn't actually matter how any of the people or involvements in your room got there, or what came with them. You may have invited them in, or they may have pushed their way in. They may be in your room because they are family, or because you think you need them. If they are in your room, one way or another their presence greatly impacts the quality of your life— *for better or for worse.*

Sometimes people gain entry into your room and bring chaos to your life, but you're not aware of it until the chaos reaches a tipping point. You may feel victimized by some of the people and stuff in your room, but this isn't about pointing fingers. It's not about blame; it's about taking an honest look at what's going on in your room, and considering what you need in the way of a remodel. You may even find yourself thinking that it's time for an extreme makeover.

Going forward, you can become vigilant and attentive to who's knocking on your door. You can learn to manage who (and what) has already gained entry. You can set better guidelines that determine who you let inside, as well as how to manage the current population and what they brought with them.

You might not be able to permanently eject people or things that are already in your room, but you can definitely—and permanently—change how those people and things occupy your space. And ultimately, change how they affect you.

The goal is for you to learn how to apply the *Who's in Your Room?* concept so that you can achieve more success and more fulfillment in all areas of your life—from your most intimate personal relationships to your professional pursuits and business ventures.

This may sound like a bold, overly ambitious assertion to make. However, if you allow the room concept to really sink in, you will become an excellent decision maker across the broad spectrum of choices you regularly face in your life. After all, life is a series of important decisions. *What should I do with my life? Who can I trust to go into business with? How do I deal with the difficult people in my life? Who should I marry? Where should I live? Where am I going?*

There are also those questions that penetrate our minds on occasion that reflect disappointment: *How did it come to this? Why did this happen? What did I do wrong? Why isn't my life working out on any meaningful level? Why doesn't it work better?*

Or perhaps things in your life are going really well, but for some reason you constantly feel like it isn't going to last. Becoming thoughtful about who's in your room will help you develop the belief that you can make it last.

Up until now, you may have been more unconscious than thoughtful about who and what you have invited into your room. Maybe you have had the thought that "life happens," and that you don't have much control over things. By applying the room concept you will discover otherwise, and this can give you a new and unambiguous framework with which to build a life that makes sense to you, and that gives you freedom.

Simply put, the room concept equips you with a highly effective process for making better choices, and therefore living the life you've always wanted.

Chapter 2

Addicted to "Yes"

You live in a fast-paced world—your cell phone constantly ringing, emails piling up, and contacts from people who all seem to want something from you: your time, your help, your involvement in their lives or in a project, and on and on. And far too often, you say yes.

Did you know that the number-one regret people have when death is closing in on them is, *"I wish I'd had the courage to live a life true to myself, rather than the life others expected of me."* Why do so many of us end up having this same regret? People in hospice care commonly reflect on a life spent saying yes too often to others, and saying no too often to themselves, or at least to what their true selves need to be fulfilled.

Here's a simple question: Do you have a hard time saying *no?* Do you have an open-door policy on allowing people to come into your life—old friends, new friends (especially on Facebook), exes, employees, relatives, "buddies," neighbors, coworkers, casual acquaintances, etc.? Do you let these people enter your life on their own terms, at their will? Do projects, commitments, To Do tasks, group events, emails and text messages, social media notifications and more intrude upon your life—

things that you never really welcomed and can't tolerate? Is it a challenge for you to focus and concentrate on a daily basis because there are so many distractions in your life?

If you answered yes to any or all of these questions, then chances are your room is seriously overcrowded and you'll never be able to live a life that's true to yourself and accomplish your goals and dreams until you learn how to get over your addiction to yes and master the art of *no*.

Why can't we say *no?* We talked to Lynne Twist about this. Lynne is the author of the best-selling, award-winning book *The Soul of Money: Transforming Your Relationship with Money and Life (W.W. Norton, 2003)*. For over four decades she has been a recognized global visionary, committed to alleviating poverty and hunger in the third world while at the same time being a voice for social justice and environmental sustainability. Lynne's on-the-ground relief work—side by side with Mother Teresa in India, in the refugee camps of Ethiopia and amidst the threatened rainforests of the Amazon—has given her a deep understanding of the world's social tapestry and of the historical landscape of the times we are living in. When we asked her why many people have a hard time saying *no*, Lynne had quite a bit to say on the subject.

"What I have come to see is that we live with a mindset

of scarcity," she told us. "This is not about what we think, but where we are thinking from, almost like viewing the world through a lens or a filter, so that everything that we see is altered by the unconscious, unexamined mindset we approach it from. Consequently, even before thinking, before deliberation or decision, we have this filter of perception that everything is scarce and we must have more.

"This condition—or mindset—of scarcity is a total trap. This is distinct from the reality in which there are people who actually don't have enough to eat, who don't have access to clean water or adequate housing, who really don't have enough. I've spent a good portion of my life working with people like that, but I'm not talking about them. I'm talking about people primarily living in affluent, First World countries, where there is this unconscious mindset that drives aberrant behavior—this unexamined belief in scarcity.

"This mindset contains three toxic myths. The first is that there is not enough—not enough time, enough money, enough energy, sex, sleep, weekends, hours in the day or night. Somehow, there is a relentless feeling that there's not enough of everything; it's become the tyranny we live with. The second half of toxic myth number one is that there is not enough to go around and someone,

11

somewhere, will always be left out. This is a mindset that is devastating and ultimately fatal. It creates an 'us' and a 'them' and legitimizes accumulating way, way, WAY more than you need to ensure that 'you and yours' are never among those left without. With this mindset, however, somebody is always going to be left out, and we are driven to make sure it isn't us.

"This idea that there's not enough to go around is a really devastating mindset that also creates a 'personal deficit' mentality, which moves you from 'there's not enough' to 'I'm not enough.' Once you arrive at 'I'm not enough' you go into a deficit relationship with yourself, a toxic state that has you living a life of constant self betrayal as you try (and fail) to prove that you are enough.

"The second toxic myth," Lynne continued, "flows directly from the first: more is better. More of anything and everything is better—more square feet in your house, more money, more cars, more planes, more this, more that. It's not that 'more' isn't sometimes a good thing, but I'm talking about the insatiable, constant obsession with getting more that actually makes *no sense.* And it's a toxic mindset, because the drive is totally unconscious. The 'more is better' mentality is constantly and overwhelmingly preached by the advertising and marketing types that tell us that we're not okay until we have more of this, that and the other thing—more hair, bigger boobs, whatever. Analysts tell us this mindset is being constantly re-emphasized, with a minimum of about 3,000 messages per day telling us we need more of something we already have or we have to get something we don't have in order to be okay. If we live in an urban area, it can be up to tens of thousands of messages a day, which is just simply overwhelming.

"So here we are, living in the richest country on earth— which has accumulated the greatest national debt in the history of the world. This is what happens when you place a greater value on outer riches than inner riches."

At this point Lynne paused, and we did too. There was a lot to contemplate, offered by one of the world's more remarkable women.

When we believe there's never enough, and that there's never going to be enough, we say "yes" as a kind of mental insurance policy. This is true not only in business and work settings, where we take on too many projects, but also with regard to friendships -- we make room for too many friends, too many social obligations, and too many commitments in our personal lives. After all, who doesn't want to be seen as "popular," with an impressive list of contacts? How many of us constantly compare ourselves with others in the drive to have the most friends on Facebook or the most followers on Twitter?

At this point, you may start to defend yourself. You may think that you don't have a scarcity mindset. How could anybody think there is a scarcity of possibilities and opportunities? Of course there isn't a shortage of possibilities—and that's a problem. When we talk with brain scientists, great coaches and mentors in all fields of human endeavor, we are told that greatness takes focus. So why does it seem as if our modern world is organized around a conspiracy of distraction by possibilities? Well, because in a world of scarcity we believe that more possibilities offer us safety.

It can take a while to get good at separating a possibility that is simply a distraction from a possibility that is actually a good opportunity. Most of us (though we protest otherwise) make decisions based on emotion, which we then justify with a litany of reasons generated by our supposedly rational mind. The resulting dissonance is quite stressful and can drive us to bizarre behaviors!

No one ever does anything for absolutely no reason, whether or not they're aware of the reason. When you find yourself behaving in ways that are at odds with your consciously stated objective, ask yourself, "What must I believe to be true for my current behavior to make sense?" We suggest that when you look behind a conflicted *yes*, you'll find a concern that if you were to say *no* you could lose something of value. You may think a *no* will cost you a friendship or a business relationship, that if you say *no* to what may be a good opportunity you will never be offered another one. Most of us hate to feel that we might be missing out. Underlying these concerns is a presumption of scarcity. But did you know that enduringly successful people say no many times more than they say *yes?*

Tim Cook, the CEO of Apple, once said in an interview that he was really proud of all the things at Apple that they said *no* to. He asserted that saying *no* was harder—and more important—than saying *yes.* He emphasized, "Focusing is about saying no," Cook emphasized. Apple said *no* to making personal digital assistants—in the 1990s, that is. It said *no* for years to making a phone—until it said *yes.* Many of us wanted a Newton2 or a netbook, but Apple wouldn't make one. It just didn't fit into their vision or where they were going. Steve Jobs said at the time that they could not hit the netbook price point and provide people with a great experience—so he gave us the iPad instead, and once again changed the game. All the big players have since pulled out of the netbook business, because the user experience was in fact universally awful. Products like the iPod, iPhone and iPad—which revolutionized the music, mobile, and PC industries, respectively—all focus on simplicity and say *no* to many of the bells and whistles hyped by the competition.

If you happen to be an entrepreneur or a CEO, your customers, investors, friends, and even random strangers will want you to do things that may sound exciting and even lucrative. That doesn't mean you should do them. It's hard, but you must learn to say *no* way more than you say *yes*. It will keep you focused and within the territory of your vision. And even if you are not an entrepreneur, you are CEO of your own life, and learning to say *no* will allow you to live a life true to yourself, rather than the life other people expect (or demand) of you.

In the next chapter you will meet your new best friend, who will help you say *no*.

Chapter 3

You Need a Doorman!

Take a moment to imagine what it would be like to have your very own "doorman" in life, someone who intimately knows everything he needs to know about you in order to act as your resident gatekeeper—a guardian of all things good for you. He allows into your room all that will enrich your life—people, projects and involvements—and makes sure that negative influences stay out. He even possesses a sixth sense about whatever shows up at your door, knowing right away whether it will hurt or help you in the long run, even if you don't know it yet. Note that I'm not actually referring to a real person here. Rather, this is a virtual doorman who patrols the entrance to the room of your life.

Your doorman is really clear and knowledgeable about your personal values, about what matters to you. He knows what things you are deeply passionate about and is committed to supporting only the best for you. Your doorman will not let anybody into the room of your life who does not support your values or passions.

Of course, you will have to brief your doorman before you put him to work. This means you have to get really clear within yourself about your values and what matters to you. You need to recognize what it is you are deeply passionate about and make a commitment to developing your potential. Until you do, you will not be able to tell the difference between an opportunity and a distraction.

To do his job well, your Doorman will need you to provide him with a set of values—guidelines that he will use to determine who (or what) is allowed to enter into the room of your life or business. Ultimately, these guidelines directly relate to how you want to live and what you hope to achieve. They also have a substantive influence on all those things that make you, well, *you*— whether you're fit or fat, liked or disliked, whether you attract good opportunities or not. They can reflect whether you're accelerating or decelerating in life, whether you have enriching relationships or meaningless ones with people who take advantage of you, whether you're married to your soul mate or someone who doesn't "get you." They can help determine whether you live in a cluttered trailer or the home of your dreams, whether you're happy or depressed, whether you're in debt or financially sound, whether you enjoy or hate your job, whether you struggle with the weight of too much stress or not, and so on.

Earlier we mentioned that you could alter how much past mistakes affect you today and in the future. You can relegate them to an out-of-focus section, way in the background, and move into sharp focus in the foreground the elements of your past that can be building blocks for the future you want. As you and your virtual doorman work together to build your desired future, you essentially transform your relationship with the past. Asking, "Who is in my room and what are they doing here?" helps you to mentally and emotionally move people and projects from the foreground to the background. Those troublesome people and events that have had starring roles in the story of your life become mere dots in the distant background. Consider building a very large closet—maybe a basement or even a dungeon—to put away the most undesirable elements that ended up in your room. In this way, you create space for what you actually want to be featured up front and personal in the foreground of your life.

You don't have to put up with drama and intruders in your room if you don't want to. Your Doorman works with you to say *no* and to avoid giving equal weight and attention to everything in your room. But you have to be vigilant. You will need to work with your Doorman on a daily basis. Again, this comes from developing and maintaining a keen understanding of your values, which will dictate how your Doorman will do his job and manage access to your room.

The process of "hiring" your Doorman is straight-forward. First, you need to create your list of values. Then, figure out your list of deal-breakers—personalities and projects that are automatically denied entry to your room. (You can accomplish these tasks with the help of the exercises provided in Chapter 24, page 136, *What Are Your Values?* at any time.)

We also strongly recommend that you read Chapter 23, page 131, *How Will You Treasure the Breaths You Have Left?*, before you create your list of values and hire your doorman. This piece by #1 *New York Times* best selling author Geneen Roth has had a great impact on us, and we think it will on you too. In fact, if you are the kind of person who likes to peek at the back of a book before you get too far in, consider reading Chapter 23 next and then return to Chapter 4.

Chapter 4

Thought-Style Matters

Let's talk a bit more about the implications of the idea that whoever and whatever comes into the room of your life is there with you forever. Once again, it isn't literally true that the people who gain entrance to your room are physically with you for the rest of your life. What we are saying is that whoever comes into the room of your life becomes incorporated into the current of energy that turns the windmill of your mind—forever!

We're all limited by what we are capable of perceiving. Our perceptions are skewed by our passions and fears— and for the most part we can't help but think that everyone else cares about, responds or reacts to the same things we care about, respond or react to. We're limited by what we've experienced, by the realities we grew up in—by the asserted "facts" that dominated our world, even if we (or others) made up a good part of it all.

In a similar vein, Steve Jobs famously said, "Successful people think different." We half-jokingly said to our publisher one day, "Let's do a book called *Thought-Styles of the Rich and Famous.*" He was underwhelmed. But if you actually want to isolate the single most powerful trait that separates the men and women who live wonderful

21

lifestyles from those who mostly don't, then it would be this concept called *thought-style*. We define *thought-style* as the meaning-making process that shapes our thoughts, feelings and behaviors.

We certainly could do a whole book on thought-styles, and notably a few people have, mostly using the term *mindset*. Carol Dweck, the Lewis and Virginia Eaton Professor of Psychology at Stanford University, authored a wonderfully useful book titled *Mindset* that we can heartily recommend. In it, she introduces the idea of making a simple distinction when it comes to mindsets, and proposes two categories. One category she calls a *fixed mindset* and the second category a *growth mindset.*

The book goes on to convincingly demonstrate that emotional and material success in life requires that we view and interpret our experiences in life from the viewpoint of a growth-oriented mindset. We prefer the term *thought-style* to *mindset* because *mindset* implies that the way your mind functions is set (as in stone), but it isn't. Carol makes a compelling case for this liberating reality.

If you are curious to know what kind of thought-style you have, then respond to the statements below. Simply respond to each statement with either "I mostly agree" or "I mostly disagree."

1. My intelligence is a basic quality I was born with and I can't change that very much.

2. People can learn new things, but they really can't change how intelligent they are.

3. No matter how much intelligence I have, I can always enhance it quite a bit.

4. People can always change how intelligent they are.

5. I am a certain kind of person, and there isn't much that I can do to really change that.

6. No matter what kind of person I am, I can always change substantially.

If you mostly agree with statements 1, 2, and 5, and mostly disagree with statements 3, 4, and 6, then you have a fixed thought-style, and you have a problem. If, on the other hand, you mostly disagree with statements 1, 2, and 5, and mostly agree with statements 3, 4, and 6, then you have a growth thought-style and a lot of opportunities for a successful life.

If it appears that you have a fixed thought-style, don't panic. Contrary to popular belief in the matter, there is an ever-expanding body of scientific research on how the brain works that establishes that we can continue to enhance our intelligence (complexity of mind) and our style of thinking throughout our entire lives! This fact means that the concepts of *who's in your room?* and having a doorman are truly life-changing, if you put them to work for you.

If you have a fixed thought-style, it is an unfortunate gift from the people who crowded into your room in the formative stages of your life. Tragically, often with the best of intentions, parents, other family members, teachers, and friends unwittingly conspired to ensure that early on in your life you became the unhappy owner of a fixed thought-style. It may seem to be totally unfair that these people dominated the real estate of your room during these early years. And it *would* be tragically unfair, if there were nothing you could do about it today. However, you can do something about it. More than something—you can do *a lot* about it.

Researchers have learned a great deal in recent years about how we learn and change. Previously, popular wisdom held that you had to deal with the past before you could grow into the future you wanted. You had to break old, negative patterns and eliminate negative beliefs before you could have the life that you desired. If you have tried dealing with a bad habit head on by trying to break it, you've probably found that this tactic doesn't work very often, because habits are really tough to break. The problem lies inside our brains. While the brain is really skilled at building new circuits of learning, it is awful at unbuilding them. No matter how hard to break a bad habit, it is still there inside your head, wired into your brain (i.e., in your room), just waiting to be activated.

What can you do about it? The answer is simply to ignore the bad habit or negative belief and put your energy to work building a new habit or useful belief to override the old one. This is the functional equivalent of moving stuff from the foreground of your room to deep into the background, creating space for it to be mindfully replaced by what it is you do want in your life.

The power of the "Who's in your room?" idea and the "Doorman principle" is that by utilizing them you can focus your energy on bringing people and ideas into your room that will support the future you desire. Then the elements of the past that you strive to be free of simply fade away into the background. These principles are powerfully creative. Think of everyone in your room as a potential teacher and mentor. Some may be shining examples for you, while others might serve as a terrible warning.

Ultimately, you should realize that if you do the work, you can replace your fixed thought-style with a growth thought-style. And if you already have a mostly growth thought-style, you can continue to develop its power. The way you do this is to add a condition to the list of values that you use to train your doorman: the condition that anybody allowed to enter and occupy space in the foreground of your room must possess a growth thought-style.

Your doorman should be able to recognize these people for you, because they live life with the belief that no matter what level of intelligence a person is born with, they can continue raise it throughout their lifetime. They celebrate their own and other people's ability to learn and change. They live as advocates for the actualization of the human potential, and are committed to developing a self-transforming mind—in other words, they are diligent in recognizing the limitations and biases of their current ways of thinking and actively seek out new ways of thinking to free the human spirit. Fill the foreground of your room with people like this, and it will absolutely change your life.

Chapter 5

Learning to Say "No"

In the hustle and bustle of today's fast-paced world, scored by the ringing of cell phones and inundating chatter of texts and emails, amid the demands for time and attention by friends, family, and business partners, it becomes all too easy to be pulled down into the vortex of a confusion, to feel overwhelmed, and—this is the really big one—to lose your way.

Stop for a moment, then, and think back to the last time you felt calm, centered, and in control, as opposed to pestered, bothered, and over-committed. Think about when you last felt that you had enough of that most elusive of commodities: time. When you last felt true peace of mind.

Libby's Story

Elizabeth "Libby" Scheele is a Minnesota artist who found her creative wings had been clipped by having too much going on. What was worse, she realized that she was the one responsible. She simply could not say "no" to others. She decided that she needed to do something about it. Here, she tells her story.

When I didn't have a guardian at the door, my room was like the waiting area in the ER. I was always admitting one emergency after another. I had become addicted to yes, and learning to say *no* was very difficult. Without a doorman, I found myself constantly performing triage in an attempt to restore a sense of order to my life.

Being a good nurturer is one of my core values. As I tried to live up to this value, I often felt overwhelmed. I was taking in too many people and projects and my own work suffered. I'd get a burst of creative energy, but I would be so busy that I couldn't be present to it. I couldn't respond, so whatever that energy might have become would be lost.

Originally, I thought that as soon as I announced the beginning of my creative journey, everybody in my life would magically step forward and say, "Okay Libby, your schedule is cleared. We won't ask anything of you." Needless to say, that didn't happen.

Given my need to be a nurturer, people are very comfortable asking me for help—especially my husband. And I love to be available for him. I also love to be available for my family and my community. At the same time, I really feel there are creative things that are supposed to come through me and into this world, and I absolutely have to make time to do them.

Today, using the concept of the room, I practice making the distinction between opportunities and distractions. I have taught myself to take it one event at a time, with the understanding that just because I am related to someone, and just because I have spent a huge amount of time with him or her over the years, it doesn't mean that person or their project is automatically front and center in my room.

For me, this is a total change. Before, I always felt I was moving away from things, trying to escape to a place for myself. Now I feel I'm moving toward something. I have set up my schedule and established my boundaries, and I treasure my time. I simply let others know that I am moving toward a goal, and I need this time for me. It feels different—it feels like I have earned their respect. As a consequence, I actually feel closer to people, rather than feeling like we have moved farther apart.

Now, when people give me an invitation or offer me what they believe is an opportunity, I listen to them very carefully. Then I tell them how much I appreciate their thoughtfulness; I always make sure they know that I am grateful for the offer. Some of these people I let into my room, but I tell them they cannot bring the project with them I also let them know they have to be very quiet if they are going to be in my room. It's not as if I am dumping friends or excommunicating anybody. I am simply establishing boundaries, so that I have time that is my time, to express my passion through projects that profoundly matter to me.

In the past, if I got really busy I just would ignore email, phone calls, and text messages. This is not a very kind thing to do—people start to make up stories in their minds about why this is happening to them, why they are being ignored. Now, I make a point of answering those emails, calls, and texts, even if I have to say "no." And I am always very mindful of being kind when I decline a project, meeting, or social event.

My friends understand what deeply matters to me. They feel that by graciously accepting and acknowledging that I need to reserve time for my projects, they are actually supporting my dreams and aspirations, and in so doing they are also being a good friend.

My brain used to be like the local supermarket—open 24/7. Today, I find there is more space in my life, and a lot less chattering in my mind. I am no longer trying to juggle so many different lives. I am more focused on my own life, and it feels wonderful. And yet, I continue to feel very connected to the people in my life.

I just spent a couple hours with my 87-year-old neighbor. I play cribbage with him every week. Today he wanted to play one more game and I said to him, "Leonard, I really have to go home right now—the light is perfect and I need to finish the painting I'm working on, but I will see you on Sunday." And he was fine with that.

Before, I would've said, "Well, okay, one more game" and resented it, because on some level, I believed I was keeping him alive. And I would think, "If I don't play one more game with him, he might pass away faster," which is all part of this fear I have that if I don't take care of people, bad things will happen. Now I'm realizing that they may be just fine on their own.

I am so grateful that I dealt with my fear and put into practice this idea of who's in my room and trained my doorman as my gatekeeper. Now I have this good habit—a simple question that I always ask myself: "Is this person in my room?" or "Is this project in my room?"

When you regain that heightened sense of control over your own life—the personal power that Libby began to feel over the constant calls, requests, and demands made on her time and attention—then you can regain your purpose, see the way forward, and (gasp) weigh what really matters to you. As a consequence, you start getting things done again—the things that really matter.

You may need to take a moment or three to recall what your mission was and re-center in your purpose, but don't hesitate to take the time out to do so. It can be invaluable, as you will see when you peer into Peter's story.

Chapter 6
Let Your Mission Fill Your Room

You have no doubt heard about the concept of a "purpose-driven life." But when was the last time you stripped aside all the busyness and looked really hard at what drives you? What is it that makes you tick? What are the core values upon which you build your happiness? And shouldn't this be the driving force behind the decisions you and your doorman make about who and what gets into your room?

Peter's Story

> *For as long as he could remember, Peter had enjoyed cooking for others. From a young age, he had made plans to someday own a restaurant. Providing people with the experience of beautiful, delicious food was his way of contributing to the world and spreading love and good cheer. However, after following his dream and establishing a café and catering company in Denver, he hit a serious speed bump and found himself faltering. His small establishment wasn't turning a decent profit anymore, and he had a high turnover rate among his employees. Here, he talks about making personal change a priority and how he was then able to turn things around.*

The word was that I had become one of the worst people to work for in town. Moody. Bossy. Pretty much a jerk. At the same time, a competitor who opened up down the street was taking away my customers. Worse, working was no longer a source of pleasure to me. In the beginning, I used to smile a lot. But as the difficulties mounted, I found that I wasn't smiling as much. Work had become a chore, and I wanted to change that.

As I thought about this idea of who was in my room, what I really wanted to figure out was, "Why do I do what I do?"

After I thought about it awhile I said to myself, "I guess I want to be a success." But then I wondered, what does that even mean?

"I want to have the number one café and catering company west of the Mississippi," I said, with the most spirit I'd shown in a while. A goal to be proud of, for sure.

Then I thought about it some more. Okay, let's say I do become number one. The magazines rank me at the top, the mayor gives me the key to the city, and I've got places like Yelp and Zagat on my side to prove it. When it's all over and I pass on to the next world, my tombstone reads, "He Ran the Number One Café West of the

Mississippi." I took a deep breath and mulled that over, while looking around the inside of my café. Then I asked myself: "How would that make me feel?"

Well, I discovered that I actually felt worse! Not a good thing. So I asked myself why I get out of bed and go to work every day.

I told myself, "I'd like to have the money to send my kids to college. I'd like to live in a nice house and to travel the world. Wait! That somehow sounds shallow. I certainly don't want my tombstone to read, "He Lived the Life of Luxury."

I went through this exercise a few more times, and each time I abandoned my conclusion almost as quickly as I formed the words.

So I took a few long, long walks, and I thought hard about this conundrum. I realized that what I really had to do was think about what my ultimate mission was. What am I all about? What got me up in the morning way back in the beginning, when I was loving it? I knew this had to come from me, and no one else. Not my wife, not my kids, not my mother, not my employees.

I thought about the question all night long, and finally it hit me. You might think the answer I discovered sounds lame, that it doesn't seem profound enough. But here it is:

I wanted to be a joy-giver. I wanted to bring joy to people who eat my food, sit at my tables, and invite my catering service into their home or business. I wanted my family to see me as someone who brings joy to the world.

If my tombstone someday says, "He brought joy to everyone who sat at his table," that would be great. That would be success.

It wasn't about all the rankings or the accolades. It was about bringing joy to people. That was all that mattered.

Once I had my insight and knew my ultimate mission, I began constructing my values in more detail, with an eye on fulfilling that purpose. I realized I'd been operating from a place of fear. Consequently, my room wasn't filled with the people and things that would help me live up to this purpose of spreading joy. My doorman and I had better start getting busy!

Within four months, my business experienced a satisfying turnaround. Old customers started coming back. Good employees stuck around. A new manager, one who was fully aligned with my values, was in place. I didn't beat myself up like I used to. And even on busy days, I'd sit with customers and ask them about what changes they wanted to see, or if there was anything I

could add to the menu to make their bellies happier—
and lives more joyful.

Now, I feel far more engaged in life each day—in the
process of learning, in the pleasure of cooking, catering,
and serving, and in virtually every part of life that
matters outside of my business, too.

It's possible to get so swept away by the everyday details
of life that you lose track of the things that matter
most to you. This is the time to rethink your goals and
decisions, and then maybe give your room an extreme
makeover and train your doorman very well.

Chapter 7

Goals and Decisions

All of your values and deal-breakers factor into your goals. The reverse is true as well—your goals should help define your values and deal-breakers, and thus help determine who's allowed into your room and who isn't. Take, for example, the goal of making more money. It makes sense that if you aim to increase your income, then you don't want to surround yourself with people who are constantly struggling with their finances or who don't care about advancing in their careers.

If you desire to have a happy, nurturing relationship with your partner or spouse, then you don't want to be around people who are not themselves in happy, healthy relationships. If you are looking to start a business, then it helps to spend time with other entrepreneurs and like-minded individuals who enjoy the thrill of taking those kinds of calculated risks in life rather than be someone's employee. And if you aim to lose 20 pounds, then you should surround yourself with others who make health a priority and who enjoy a fit lifestyle.

Goals and values go hand in hand. The power of developing and refining these with your own doorman over the course of your lifetime can make a huge difference in how your life turns out. Only when you are living your values and surrounding yourself with like-minded people can you become clear about your life's purpose while also gaining clarity on your goals and objectives. As you bring people and projects into your life that fully align with your purpose, values, and objectives, those positive decisions will compound over time and your life will gain momentum.

However, you also need to be on guard, because the opposite is true as well. If you pay no attention to the type of people and things that you allow into your life, operating in random fashion—the way most people do—then your life will become chaotic and unmanageable.

When you start to become successful and are granted respect by others, the difference between building enduring success and losing momentum is rarely just about your skills, talents, or track record. It's also about having a room that's carefully guarded and maintained, so it remains fully reflective of your authentic motives and intentions. Unfortunately, it's easy in today's culture to lose your way. As Mae West once famously quipped, "I used to be Snow White, but I drifted."

Measuring things can help you keep track of your progress on the long journey toward your goal, but it won't tell you if you're headed the right direction. It's important to start with the end in mind, but it could become a dead end if you're in a huge hurry to set a goal without checking in to make sure that the goal is an aligned outcome of living your values and pursuing your purpose.

The goal-setting process is both powerful and dangerous, because it can make you effective at achieving objectives—to "take the hill," as they say—without any assurance that it's the right mountain for you to climb. Goals have no intrinsic meaning. You must invest meaning in them. Goals don't come with a built-in guarantee that you'll benefit by reaching them or enjoy the process of getting there, nor do they affirm that you're on the right track. Goals, by their nature, don't necessarily require inspiration as much as they do perspiration and the sheer pragmatic effort to get things done.

The whole point of clarifying your goals to align with your values is to ensure that you live a purpose that satisfies your needs, not just your wants. If you drift and chase a false purpose, your life will eventually come apart, as did Peter's did.

So ask yourself: *Are my goals aligned with my values? Am I living with a true sense of purpose? Is my doorman selecting and inviting in people and projects that reflect clarity about my values and purpose?* Only you can answer these questions. And it is only when you answer them that you can truly shape the room that will define your life and your ultimate success.

Chapter 8
Your Room Should Be Comfortable, So Why Isn't It?

The idea of thinking of your life in the context of the room is that it's one way for you to get outside yourself and be more objective. Sounds like circular logic, doesn't it? The point is to pry apart what drives you, motivates you, and allows you to have an enjoyable life. You don't have to be constantly examining these things—but you need to have a steady awareness of them to be more relaxed and present in your life. Allow yourself to savour what the true you chooses to have in your life, with the help of your doorman.

Mark's Story

Mark McKergow is a global pioneer in applying Solutions Focus ideas to organizational and personal change. He has an MBA and a PhD in physics, and writes frequently on systemic thinking and assorted other subjects. Mark describes himself as a recovering nuclear physicist. We present this piece in Mark's own words with his inner scientist intact.

Have you ever been walking along and suddenly become aware that there's a stone in your shoe? Me too. You don't know where it came from, or how it got in there, or indeed exactly where it is. You just know that your foot is starting to hurt.

If you're like me, you'll continue walking for a bit, hoping that maybe the stone will get out the way it came in, or shift to a less painful spot, or maybe you'll just get used to it. And, of course, none of these things happen. The hurt just gets more annoying, and more intense. After a while it becomes the only thing you can think about, consuming more and more of your attention, until if a genie came along and offered you a single wish you'd immediately shout, "Just get this blankety-blank stone out of my shoe!"

Of course, with a real stone in a real shoe, you eventually learn to just stop, take your shoe off, empty out the stone and carry on. In the world of the room concept, it's not so simple. Once someone has entered your room, they're there for good. You can't just stop and shake them out like an annoying stone, however much you'd like to. By now you have probably realized that this "they're there for good" concept is not just a crazy idea—it's actually a very accurate and incisive reflection of how our lives really operate.

Philosopher, social constructionist and professor Kenneth Gergen of the Taos Institute has spent decades studying at how we construct and live our lives, not as isolated individuals but as relational networks of interaction and meaning. He contends that not one word comes from your mouth that doesn't have its origin in some past conversation or relationship. So, it's not just you who is speaking. Your words are the outcome of a thousand conversations of which you've been a part. Gergen claims that all your actions, the way you walk, interact, and even think, is imported from previous relationships.

So it really is as if you are carrying around everyone you've ever interacted with. You can't unscramble an egg, and similarly you can't un-interact your life.

Of course, you don't carry around everyone you've ever met with equal weight. A lot depends on the level, intensity, duration, and context of your relationships. You carry around the other person's words, gestures, and even expressions. Sometimes you can trace back where they came from and sometimes you can't, but you know they came from somewhere.

Sometimes, of course, people come into your room and things turn sour. Your doorman can help you make smarter choices about who to let in and who to keep at a (significant) distance. Your doorman is going to be your best advisor from now on. But what about the folks who are already in your room, who came in before you engaged the doorman and are now cluttering up your space? In particular, what about those individuals who are like that annoying stone in your shoe?

First of all, don't beat yourself up about it. If you'd never put yourself in a position to have different relationships, you'd basically be reduced to a life of breathing, digestion, and walking on all fours, as Gergen puts it. Stuff happens. It's how you deal with it that determines what happens next.

In my own life, I have experienced the pain and misery of having someone in my room who was making things very difficult for me. After several years of fruitful working relations with this person, it seemed that things were becoming more and more one-sided, with a lot of taking going on and very little giving in return. When I tried to raise the matter, I was always told that there was a "good reason" for the particular issue, and that this was a "special case." The trouble was that pretty much every case was like this, and I became more and more concerned. Finally I lost my patience and brought the relationship to as quick and clean an end as I could.

And guess what? I was the LAST person to figure out what was happening. When I mentioned it to my partner, she said, "Aha! So you've finally seen it! I've been telling you for ages to watch out for this, but you never wanted to hear it."

She was right, of course. I didn't want to hear it. But in the end all kinds of pain ensued, and it was some time before my life and business could resume, and at a considerable cost in time, effort and intellectual capital. However, I also learned a lot through this relationship that I am now grateful for—about writing, editing, stagecraft, and proper business arrangements, all things that I use often.

So a hint for your doorman: Listen to what your long-term friends and companions are trying to tell you. Seek their advice; be open to their views. When you get a tiny twinge of feeling that "this isn't going well," learn to look around and discuss it with those you really trust. There's an old saying in military circles: "Once is happenstance, twice is coincidence, third time it's enemy action." I suggest you get your radar out at "twice"—if something happens more than once, be aware and on the lookout for signs in all directions.

Here's a thought for you. Just as a person is in your room, you are in theirs. What did they appreciate and learn from you? How might this be useful to them? At best, they may have been changed radically for the better by their experience with you. It's never too late to have a happy (or at least relaxed and comfortable) ending to your story.

––––––––––––––––––

Isn't one of the main reasons you are considering this room idea right now because you are feeling crowded and uncomfortable, as if you had, as Mark puts it, an emotional stone in your shoe? In the next chapter, we'll get a different perspective on how and why you should be more selective about who enters your room in the first place.

Chapter 9

Making Better Choices: Being More Selective

When you (or your doorman) say *yes* or *no*, it should not be an automatic response. You can get a robot for that.

What should actually happen is a deliberate process, in which your values are factored into each decision. When your doorman knows what those values are the process moves more quickly, and that can make a big difference when one of your values is your time.

Dr. Deb's Story

> *Dr. Debra Olson-Warford operates Quantum Health Chiropractic in Lancaster, California. Dr. Deb first came to chiropractic care seeking relief from 12 years of intense hip pain that left her barely able to walk. After finding relief, and what she regards as the priceless gift of being able to resume a normal life, she is now a gifted human and animal Chiropractor. Here, she shares her story.*

I used to accept new patients in my business whether or not I was certain there was a good fit. Now, when my team and I are interviewing a prospective patient to see whether we can partner with them to make a positive contribution to their health, one *no* vote from a team member cancels out all the *yes* votes. If we decide not to invite a person to become part of our practice family, I guide them to a practitioner who I think would be a better fit.

When a potential new patient walks through the door, we gently let them know right up front that we may not be able to accept them as a patient. It all depends on a number of things. I do corrective care, so one of my criteria is if they don't have a problem that I believe I can help them with, then I don't accept them as a patient. Also, if their energy doesn't feel right for our office, we would be concerned that it would disrupt the human energy of our practice, so we might not want to accept them as a patient.

Most people who walk into our office remark on how it feels like entering a healing space. Usually my patients are in no hurry to leave—after they have received their care, they often want to hang out for a while and chat because of the very happy healing energy present. It just feels really good to be in our space.

Some days I help over 100 patients. We have to make sure that everybody is energetically protected, because everybody's energy affects everyone else. Consequently, we want to make sure that we maintain an optimum healing energy in our office throughout the day. We get great results with our corrective care, and I believe that part of the reason is the energy in our office is protected from negative influences. Carefully selecting the people we accept as patients is critical to safeguarding this space and its healing energy.

You can just feel people's energy. Yesterday I was giving a small class on how people can be an advocate for their own health care. There was one lady present whose energy was very negative. She didn't say a word, but I could tell from the way she carried herself—from her body posture to the expression on her face—that her energy was not aligned with the spirit of our practice. When it was time for me to go over her x-rays with her I respectfully suggested that another doctor would be more appropriate to her needs and provided a referral. I was not rude to her in any way—I was very compassionate about it—and she felt cared for. I believe it is always important to be kind to people; kindness is healing.

Of course, there is a difference between someone who comes in the door grouchy because they are in pain and somebody whose presence just doesn't feel right. By paying attention to this difference, I can sense whether or not it's appropriate for somebody to be part of our practice.

People ask me, "Isn't it scary to turn away new patients, particularly in difficult economic times?" For me it isn't scary at all. I have learned that if I really safeguard the healing energy in the office, and refer potential patients who I don't feel would be a good fit to another chiropractic office, we actually get a greater number of new patients.

It's been an amazing change. Before I learned about the concept of who's in your room and how place a doorman on duty, we would typically have three or four new patients a month coming in to see me. Today, we had 21 new patients just like week apply to become a member of our practice family. On average, I'd say we have at least quadrupled the number of new patients we see each month. Additionally, I have had patients who had dropped out of care return and reengage with us. Some patients have said they keep coming back not only for the treatments, but also because it is so uplifting to be in our office.

Now, referring a possible new patient elsewhere is not scary at all. I know that when I am clear about my values and live by them in my daily life, other people who have similar core values are attracted to me. Because of that, my life has gotten better. I have become a more productive and more effective doctor. Since I have a chiropractic office, I could rephrase the question and ask "Who's in your waiting room?" I have also trained my staff to be very good "doormen." The results have being truly remarkable, both in terms of patient outcomes and financial results. I am thrilled.

Being more selective is what the room concept is all about, but the reason for selection or rejection is sometimes determined by whether you're the right person to do someone else the most good. As we shall see in the next chapter, the room idea not only works with people, or with projects that seek to enter your life, but also with the things that keep you afloat, like money.

Chapter 10
Who's In Your Wallet?

All of us lean on someone every once in awhile for advice. You probably talk to close friends about your job, relationships, or even money. Perhaps especially money. Just like people and projects, financial matters can be a big factor in your room. And when there are ripples in your financial pond, you find yourself hoping there's a tsunami on the way.

Matt's Story

> *Matt Weinstein, a founding president of an innovative California team-building consulting company, travels internationally as an award-winning speaker and was featured on a PBS special called "Fun Works!" In the story below, he relates how he suddenly learned that everything he had saved for years had been wiped out.*

A few years ago I was on vacation in Antarctica with my old college roommates. It was not exactly a laid back week or two at the seaside! We had a spectacular voyage on a Russian icebreaker, watched penguins frolic, gaped as icebergs floated by like extraordinary works of art, and observed breathtaking scenery everywhere we looked.

About halfway through the sea voyage I was paged over the loudspeaker to go to the bridge for a satellite phone call. I thought I knew what it was about. I had been working with a speaker's bureau on a series of keynote speaking engagements, and they were going to contact me if the negotiations hit a snag. I went dashing up the stairs to receive my call, because I knew that satellite phone calls cost 10 dollars a minute. At the time I remember thinking to myself, "This is kind of fun—doing business from Antarctica!"

When I picked up the phone, it was not the speaker's bureau. Instead, it was my wife, Geneen. Her voice was calm and steady, but her first few words turned my life upside down. "Bernie Madoff has been arrested," she said. "His entire fund is a complete scam."

What she did not add, but both of us knew very well in that moment was that we had just lost our entire life savings.

Geneen and I had started out with nothing, worked really hard for 30 years, and built up a healthy retirement fund. Ten years before, we had invested that money with Bernie Madoff. He was a superstar investor, the former chairman of the NASDAQ. What could go wrong? Now, in an instant, it was all gone.

I felt punched in the stomach. A wave of anxiety rolled over me. It turned out that Madoff had stolen 18 billion dollars (not all of that was mine, mind you!).

Geneen and I had a moment of panic together. We didn't know if we would be able to afford to stay in our house or have to move. We didn't know what would happen. We talked anxiously for a few more minutes until one of us (probably her) had the presence of mind to say, "You know what, Sweetheart, we are no longer the kind of people who can afford to talk on the satellite telephone at 10 dollars a minute!" So we hung up.

As soon as I put the receiver down, my hand gone clammy, the next wave of fear washed over me. Wherever I have traveled in the world, I've been able to return home in times of crisis. But this was Antarctica — they weren't going to turn the boat around for me!

I finished out the rest of the trip, but the scenery had gone flat, more ominous than thrilling. The food I ate had no taste. Geneen and I were finally reunited 10 days later. We knew for certain at that point that Bernie Madoff had stolen our money; it was up to us to make sure that he didn't steal the rest of our lives as well. As the philosopher Joseph Campbell so beautifully put it, sometimes "we must be willing to let go of the life we have planned so as to have the life that is waiting for us."

I got back to work as soon as I could — I needed to work as much as possible to start earning some money. For the past 40 years, I've been teaching people about building community through laughter and play and fun. But in order to authentically talk about the power of laughter and play, I had to get back in touch with the possibility of laughter and play in my own life, in spite of the disastrous circumstances.

That process really accelerated my healing from the situation, because I was able to discover that even in the most difficult of times, we all still have inside us the possibility of joy and play and passion for life. Joy, fun and celebration are an intrinsic part of what it means to be human.

My wife, Geneen Roth, is an author, and she went back to completing her latest book, *Women Food and God*. Both of us were on fire with creative projects. Although our finances were decimated, we had made peace with it and were moving on; we were happy in our work and full of life and excitement.

We felt closer to each other than ever before in our marriage. We had come to a place of basic trust, that whatever life had in store for us we were going to be fine with it. We didn't need some fairy godmother to come into our lives and wave her magic wand and change things around… but it happened anyway.

Oprah read *Women Food and God* and loved it, and wrote about it in O *Magazine*. She had Geneen as a guest on her radio show, and then devoted two complete Oprah TV shows to the book. As a result, *Women Food and God* became a huge #1 *New York Times* bestseller. As nearly as quickly as we had lost all our money, it all came back. As one of our close friends said at the time, "Well, you weren't poor for very long!"

We were delighted to be prosperous once again, yet we had come to realize that material wealth was a bonus for us, not something essential to life. Experiencing a major financial setback like that had helped us to change our relationship with money. We learned to hold on to it less tightly, to be more generous with it once we had it again, and to see that there was something essential in our lives and our relationship that had nothing to do with wealth.

I saw very clearly that you don't need to have a lot of money to feel loved and appreciated in your life. You don't need to be rich to feel connected to other people. You don't need a big stock portfolio to feel creativity, passion, and the joy of being alive every day.

The Madoff experience definitely changed the type of people I invite into my room nowadays. A few years before I had ever heard of Madoff, I had been ripped off by my financial advisor of 13 years, who was sentenced to prison for embezzling money. Ironically, a close friend of mine came to me after that and said, "I feel so bad about what happened to you—I think I may have way for you to recoup some of your losses. I can put you into a fund that I've been in for 30 years that has never lost money. It's something I save for the people I care about, or friends who are in trouble, like you. I'm happy to offer it to you." That fund was run by—you guessed it—Madoff.

I asked myself over and over again, how could this kind of financial betrayal happen to me not once, but twice? I came to realize that for a long time I had been placing my money with "father substitutes"—people who would take care of me with respect to money, so I wouldn't have to take responsibility for my own decisions. That way I could feel special and protected, and wouldn't have to educate myself to the difficult realities of money management.

This time around I learned some basic rules of financial management, like not to invest in anything that I don't understand and to diversify, diversify, diversify. And, yes,

I have learned to shut the door on the father figures who still appeal to me, not invite them into my room to take care of me. I have been vigilant in keeping the childlike version of myself, who wants to be taken care of and have everything done for him, away from my financial decisions. More importantly, I've learned that the one trustworthy person to let into my room when it comes to financial matters is the grown-up version of myself—a version who has learned some essential financial lessons the hard way and is able to educate himself about money matters and take responsibility for his actions.

Though, of course, Oprah can drop by any time she wants.

———

You might think of your room as something that can operate on automatic pilot once you have the template – the values and guidelines – in place. But remember, you're the one who configures that automatic pilot. You have to learn to trust yourself when setting the controls, and you have to remember to stay close by in the room just in case your automatic pilot malfunctions.

Chapter 11

Are You In Your Room?

We have mentioned overcrowding in your room, no doubt a major reason that you're reading this book. You and your doorman can fix that problem, but a cautionary word here: First check to see if you are present in your room!

Joanie's Story

Joanie is Joan Emery, Stewart's wife. We've had the opportunity to watch her work as a counselor, coach, and cheerleader for people as they travel forward on their life's journey. She believes that living in your room as "perfectly you," carefully training your doorman, and living in the question of "Who's in your room?" is the most powerful transformational practice you can embrace. Here she tells a story from her journey.

My brother Stanley had just died. During most of the time he was alive, he was only barely in my room. Now that he was dead, he seemed more present in my room than at any time since we were children. I contemplated this apparent contradiction while walking my parents' dog one morning. I drifted back to when I was a little girl, to

Who's in Your Room?
The Quality of Your Life Depends on the People in Your Life

one night when I was five or six years old and getting into bed. In front of my bed there were three or four shelves, piled high with stuffed animals and dolls.

On this particular night as I looked at the shelves, one of the dolls caught my eye. I decided I wanted to bring her into bed with me, so I got out of bed, picked up my doll, climbed back in and started to cuddle her. I was about to close my eyes and happily drift off to sleep when my eye caught another doll. I thought, well, maybe I'll bring that doll in with me too, so I got out of bed again, collected the doll and got back under the covers. Then, one of my favorite stuffed animals also caught my eye and I thought, well, I could bring that stuffed animal to bed too. This process went on for quite some time, until my bed was piled high with all the dolls and stuffed animals and I was forced to sleep on the floor.

A little while later my dad came in to check on me. He saw my bed piled high with all of the stuffed animals and dolls and said, "Joan, what are you doing?" I remember saying to my dad, "I didn't want anyone to feel left out, so I just had to bring all of my animals and dolls to bed." My dad looked at me and said, "But Joan, you're sleeping on the floor because now there's no room left for you!"

This memory has stuck with me because today in my life, I make so much room for everybody else that it

61

often feels like there's no room left for me. Many times it seemed like I was not in my own room. Even if I managed squeeze my way into my own room, oftentimes it was not the real me who made it in. So in this sense, I was still not in my room.

Ever since I started living with the idea of "Who's in your room?" my journey of discovery has accelerated. The first insight was that I never want anybody to feel left out or excluded, because I don't want to feel left out or excluded myself. The next insight was that I noticed I tend to have a crowd in my room, including people that I don't particularly like, because I want so much to be liked. This felt like a downward spiral.

Another twist in all of this was to recognize that I am often motivated to do things not because of what I truly want for me, but because of what I think other people will think of me if I do them. This is just another layer of wanting people to like me. I do things out of a need to be admired and forsake myself in the process, all in order to have people think I'm a good person and let me into their room.

Even if people seem to like me, I have no idea which me they really like. Do they like the "me" that pretends to be whatever they need me to be so they will like me, or do they actually like the real me hiding under all the pretense? Since I could never be sure of the answer, I kept right on living as the pretender, further alienating me from me. On a positive note, I discovered that whenever I caught myself doing this, in that moment I could choose to behave differently and grow as a person.

I'm at a point right now in my life where I have mostly stopped doing things just to be liked and have sorted out what I truly love to do from what I do just to have people think highly of me. I keep going deeper and deeper. A metaphor comes to mind, that the process is a bit like peeling an onion—sometimes complete with the tears.

Although by now it feels like another lifetime, in my 20s I spent over five years working in the film industry. I started in New York as a production assistant on the first *Godfather* film, followed by a stint in Sicily to complete production. Then I was invited to move to Rome and continue working in the movie business. I stayed in Italy modeling and then working on the second *Godfather* movie. I loved this experience, though after five years I badly missed my friends and family back in the States. I felt it was time to go home.

When I finally arrived back in Los Angeles, I soon felt like I didn't fit in anywhere. Nothing seemed or felt real, especially me. In Italy I felt alive. Now, back home, I felt empty inside.

Then I met a man named Pete Cameron, whom I talked to about my struggle. He handed me a paper napkin on which he'd written, "You don't have to be perfect, just be perfectly you—Actualizations." My heart took a little leap of joy. What if this was actually true? That moved me to attend an Actualizations Workshop conducted by a man named Stewart Emery. I loved what it said on the napkin, and realized I had absolutely no idea how to be that. And yet that was exactly what I wanted—to be "perfectly me."

This was over 35 years ago. And while no one was asking "Who's in your room?" or talking about having a doorman in any structured way back then, a core idea of the workshop was that if you wanted to change your life, you had to keep company with people committed to changing their own. I put this idea into practice and developed a whole new set of friendships among fellow travelers on the journey to becoming a freely choosing, fully alive human being.

So, in retrospect, I have been practicing the concept of "Who's in your room?" for over half my life. What a difference this has made. I have a lot more space for me in my room these days.

What I found is that for the transformative power of "Who's in your room?" to work its magic, you have to frequently ask yourself the question, "Am I in my room?" The answer is only "yes" if it is your true self in your room.

The room idea can be transforming, self-nurturing, and even healing. This can be especially true when not all the people you let into your room turn out to be the good ones.

Chapter 12
Everyone in Your Room Is Your Teacher

Everyone you have ever been close to—everyone who is in your room—can teach you something, whether they were part of a good time in your life or one of those harsh moments that we all deal with on occasion. The choice of how you handle it and what you learn from it is up to you.

In BNI, this is particularly true. Everyone in the group possesses knowledge about their respective fields and much, much more. One of the benefits of BNI that we hear from members all the time is how powerful it is to have this pool of knowledge at their disposal. By viewing the members as personal sources of information, your chapter becomes a room full of teachers who can help you succeed in your business and your life.

Cynthia's Story

Cynthia James is a strong-willed African American woman who transcended a childhood of violence and abuse to acquire two master's degrees, serve as Associate Minister at Mile Hi Church in Denver, and author such books as What Will Set You Free, *(used in workshops at women's prisons) and* Revealing Your Extraordinary Essence. *She has*

*led Vision-inspiring workshops in England and Ireland and
created and facilitated pilgrimages to Paris, Chartres and
Mary Magdalene's country in the south of France.*

When I first heard the concept of "Who's in your
room?" my whole body reverberated. I knew that I had
to pay attention. I started going through my "inner
files" and thought of many people I loved who were in
my room and many who, in retrospect, I would not have
invited in if I had been awake. Then a small thought
entered my head: "They were all your teachers." That
was followed by a more powerful thought: "Did you
really have to learn so many hard lessons?" Wow! What a
concept. I realized that I could have invited the kind of
teachers into my room who didn't need to evoke drama,
betrayal, pain, and suffering.

First, a little background on me. I was born into a family
that was far from nurturing. There was a lot of violence,
confusion, struggle, and crisis. This seemed natural at the
time, because my grandmother, mother, aunts, uncles,
and cousins were all living the same sort of life. It never
dawned on me that there were alternatives. My early
school years were filled with emotional explosions of one
kind or another. We moved a lot and making friends was
difficult for me.

My first real friend I can recall was Vernice. She lived next door and we would visit each other often. I was desperate to have a friend, so I accepted any treatment she was willing to offer. I wanted to be in her room in the worst way.

Many times she was mean, condescending or downright cruel toward me. One day, she became angry with me at school. We lived at the time in Minnesota, where the winters are extremely harsh. I believe it was below zero that day. Vernice took my coat and ran home, leaving me to walk almost a mile in the cold. When I got home I was half-frozen and deeply angry.

I walked up to her door and knocked. She opened it, and I punched her in the face with all of my strength. Her nose started bleeding and she ran into her house screaming. I walked away feeling very proud of myself for standing up to Vernice. As I think about this incident today, I realize it illustrates how I lived much of my life. I would invite people in, allow them to treat me in challenging ways and then, at some point, get fed up and create some intense experience.

The abuse and trauma I suffered early in life planted seeds within me of low self-esteem, doubt and fear-based thinking. Vernice was only one example of people who I invited into my life out of desperation. I had an intense need to be loved, seen, heard and acknowledged. I kept looking for and attracting people who then treated me badly. The interesting thing is that everyone I chose mirrored the people I attracted in my childhood. Well into my 20s, I began to realize that my life wasn't working. I knew that I was somehow involved in the dysfunction, but I didn't have a clue as to how to change it. I kept stumbling along until one day I found myself in a personal development workshop.

The leader of the workshop said, "Everything that is in your life is a reflection of what you believe you deserve." I was stunned. How could that be? How could I possibly believe I deserved to be betrayed, dishonored and manipulated? He had to be wrong. At the end of the workshop I approached the facilitator and shared my disbelief. He was kind and asked me, "Was your childhood a challenge?" I said, "Yes." He looked at me and said, "Perhaps your childhood taught you to expect bad things and your family members were unconscious teachers." My body tingled with goose bumps; I knew there was truth in what he was saying. That moment was the beginning of a great journey of self-discovery and of a quiet determination to heal those old wounds. I committed to learning to love myself and create a life that I could only dream of as a child.

I would love to tell you that this was an easy journey and that my life instantly changed once I had the revelation. However, nothing could be further from the truth. It took years of therapy, seminars, spiritual explorations and work creating more interesting experiences. I continued to "kiss frogs," hoping they were princes. I continued to put myself in situations where I felt used and misunderstood. I continued to blame others for my life's challenges.

The good news is that somewhere along the line, I actually woke up. I began to see that no one was doing anything to me. These painful experiences were the result of my inviting people into my life and never asking for what I really needed. I began to awaken sooner each time and recognize how these people and events reflected how I perceived myself and how I believed I deserved to be treated. I began to understand that it was possible to say "no," that I could choose how I wanted to live. I became aware that many times I was treating myself in the same ways that I accused others of mistreating me.

Although I would not wish my childhood pain on anyone, many of my experiences and lessons have helped guide and support me in doing the work that I do today with people and organizations. At this point in my life, I am very intentional about who is invited into my world.

Once people come into your room, they are there with you forever. All of the people that have crossed my path are still with me. Some of them are physically still in my life. We have grown together and supported each other in becoming more conscious beings. Others have moved away to discover their own life lessons. And still others I left, or asked them to leave, since I had outgrown my need for dysfunctional relationships.

Some of those old experiences and people who used to cause me difficulty occasionally crop up again, to invite me to undertake a greater exploration of how much I have really grown. A few years ago, I was feeling very excited about my life and all of the wonderful things that were happening. I was very cocky about my new-found freedom, education, and awareness. Then, within a two-week period, I ran into an old boyfriend who had left me, got a call from an acquaintance who had been dishonorable in our relationship, and was faced with a challenge with my youngest son. Each of these events required me to confront what I was feeling in the moment and decide quickly how I wanted to respond to these individuals and situations.

These incidents allowed me to see how I had grown and witness where my old behaviors still lived within me. Each one of these people mirrored back to me my expanded awareness and my ego-driven choices. I don't believe that old relationships have to come forward to test us. However, I do believe these relationships live within us and remind us of what we have chosen. Their presence in our lives and our memories influence how we currently choose to live.

Today, I am extraordinarily grateful for my life and treasure each moment. I have learned to listen to my intuition and trust my instincts. My room today is alive and active, filled with people who are dedicated to growth, committed to be change agents, and consciously love themselves and others. I have a loving husband and have created healthy relationships. We do not always agree, but respect is present and trust is ever expanding. I have a "gratitude chamber" for the people and circumstances that once served me, but are no longer necessary. It is a lovely little space where they can be comfortable. But make no mistake about it—the room is locked, and I hold the key next to my heart.

There is nothing more quiet and personal than your room when it is functioning well and in balance. But you have to be careful to say "yes" or "no" to people or projects for all the right reasons.

Chapter 13
The Unwanted Member

We all know the expression "Don't judge a book by its cover." This maxim is never more true than in the world of networking. We have talked about knowing who is in your room, but you must understand that you often don't know who is REALLY in your room.

You typically don't know who someone knows. You want to get to know who I know, and who I don't know. I am going to meet people in the future that I currently don't know, and they may be a perfect referral or relationship for you. But neither of us knows when or where that is going to happen. So the rule is to treat everyone like gold… because they are ALL potential gold for you and for others.

We believe that when you are building your network, you are also building the network of each person you accept into yours. But remember that you are building your network with people who you share values with, not just positions or professions. Many times we are hidden gold for each other, but we just don't know it yet.

A Story about Jacqueline and Paul as told by Ivan Misner and Frank De Raffele (to make things simpler we have combined Ivan and Frank to become the "I" in this story).

Jacqueline was hidden gold, but Paul didn't know that....

Two months into helping start a new BNI chapter in Scarsdale, New York, the Membership Committee met to talk about chapter growth and the kind of members we wanted in the group.

"Paul," a financial planner, said, "I think we should only focus on letting in business owners whose companies have at least 10 employees."

"That's not really what this is about," I responded. "The whole concept here is to have a diversity of professions, company sizes, business ages, ages of professionals, etc. Basically, it should be similar to the diversity we have now with our 36 members, but on a larger scale."

Paul strongly contended that what we currently had could be improved by getting "much better members in here."

"Better members?" I asked, with a cautionary raised eyebrow.

"Yes," he replied. "Take Jacqueline, for example." The hairs on the back of my neck bristled.

"She doesn't own a business," he continued, "and she's what, 21 years old? She's not going to be able to contribute very much to the chapter. We need the type of member who has owned a business for years, makes great money, and has a high net worth."

"Sounds to me like you're more focused on what would benefit you rather than the group," I replied. "Paul, if you're worried about the money thing, did you know that Jacqueline lives in North Salem? Have you been to North Salem?"

"Yeah, I know of it," Paul answered, his voice filled with attitude.

"Then you probably know that the houses in North Salem start at around $500,000. So somebody somewhere in her life has money, if that's your major concern. But that's not even the point. The fact that she's young and just starting her life and career is of incredible value to our group and to each of us individually. Don't you get it? She is STARTING her life. She will need everything. She will be aggressively pursuing her career, getting married, having kids, buying a car, house, insurance, and everything else you can imagine.

"This means that we are investing in futures here. She's trying to achieve success, and during this period she will be looking to the people in this room to help her. Down the road she will attribute part of her success to the help she received from all of us. That means she will be referring us out consistently now and in the future and she will have a great sense of loyalty to each of us who help her."

"Well, maybe," Paul said "But how long will that take? She may not have any REAL money for another five or more years. We could get someone who is making good money now in that position and benefit immediately, not have to wait five years to see what MIGHT happen."

"You just don't get it," I shot back. "Paul, remember, You Never Know. Besides the fact that she's a great person, a very good member, and we're keeping her," I concluded, and walked away.

Six months go by and we are having another meeting. As the president, I directed our group's attention to the referral phase of our meeting and said, "Please stand up, state your name, who your referral is for, and the quick story behind it."

Jacqueline stood up and began talking about Susan, her best friend from high school. Susan's Dad had passed away, leaving Susan, her brother and mother alone. "Then three months ago, Susan's mom died of cancer," Jacqueline continued, "and now that Susan has inherited the estate, she's not sure what to do with all the assets and asked if I knew of anyone qualified to help. I was excited to be able to refer her to Paul, because he's a great guy, so smart and good at what he does. I told her about how he helped me start a savings plan." Jacqueline went on to tell Paul that not only was she referring Susan, but that Susan's inheritance of more than $2.5 million needed managing and she needed advice on taking care of her and her brother in the process.

After the meeting was over, I was the only one left, except for two people standing towards the exit. I saw that it was Paul and Jacqueline talking, and as they were finishing up I walked over and heard Paul say, "Okay, great. No problem. I'll give her a call today and get together with her as soon as possible. Don't worry. I'll take good care of her, and thank you for the referral."

When Jacqueline walked away, I could not resist the urge to gloat a little. I walked up behind him and said loudly, "You were right, Paul, we should have GOTTEN RID OF HER six months ago!"

He dropped his head sheepishly, shook it, and said, "Oh, my gosh—I feel like such an idiot."

I couldn't help but drive the point further home. "You should, Paul. You never know. You just never know where that next referral is going to come from. Have you ever received a referral from anyone else in this group of that size?"

"Nothing even close," he replied.

I asked him if he'd ever received a two-and-a-half-million-dollar referral from anyone at all.

"No. Never," he stated.

"Never judge someone based on what you think you can get from them today. Relationships are long in the making and are about building long-term success. You never know who people are connected to or where your reputation will take you. You just never know," I said, and walked away.

Hopefully what Paul learned, and what we all need to learn from this story, is that when we are screening people to be in our room we must do it based on two things: Character and Competency. We all want competent people in our network. If someone is not good at what they do, then you will not feel comfortable in referring them out. Today, you have to be good just to be in the game. Those whose competency level is not where it needs to be will not last in business for very long.

However, character will trump competency every time. The most important aspect of screening who you let into your room is the person's character. Is that person honest, trustworthy, and a person of good business ethics? If not, no matter how well connected they are or how "successful" they are, stay away from them. Because one bad egg can smell up your whole room, and it is hard to get that smell out.

———————————

It is your room. Build with people of great character and competency. This way, you are being responsible to yourself and the others in your network. Remember, you are hidden gold to them as much as they are to you. Keep in touch with your values and choose in favor them. When we talk about trusting your heart, we're not talking about trusting your emotions. Your heart knows a deeper truth: the truth of your values.

Chapter 14
Values in Business, Values in Love

Can you really be objective about love?

The room concept is all about becoming more objective without being painful or silly about it. But as a friend of mine once said, "You can't understand great literature by using a slide rule." The same, you would no doubt agree, goes for matters of the human heart, like what drives your relationships.

There are, however, some excellent strategies you and your doorman can implement to enhance the quality of your love life! The idea of strategy and love together may not seem romantic. That's what Natalie used to think—until recently.

Natalie's Story

At the age of 25, while completing a degree in business administration, Natalie Peace started her first retail business — a Booster Juice franchise in her hometown of Kamloops, British Columbia. One year later, Natalie opened a second location of the franchise and purchased a third, building the multi-unit operation into a $2-million enterprise in a town of just 80,000 residents. As a contributing writer for

Forbes and on her personal blog PeaceandProfit.com, Natalie encourages entrepreneurs to build their businesses based on their values, her own personal secret to business success.

I believe one of reasons I've achieved success as an entrepreneur is that I clearly understood the business importance of surrounding myself with people who shared my values. I was clear about my own values, and in what I was looking for in business partners and employees. Being kind, warm, and welcoming were important team values in the quick-serve style of restaurants that I owned.

For as long as I can remember, I have believed that a well-run business can give the people working in it a chance to be fully alive and make other people's days. Over the years I have interviewed more than 600 people for positions within my organizations, and I've developed a fine-honed ability to assess whether the person sitting across from me embodied the passions and values I was looking for. I offered employment to those candidates who my senses indicated would be a good fit.

There were times when I eventually found out I'd made a mistake. Within the person's first few shifts, I would become aware that the new team member wasn't displaying the values that I thought I'd sensed in them.

If that was the case, I didn't find it difficult to share with the person what I needed from them in order to continue our relationship. If the individual couldn't be what the team and the enterprise needed, I was at ease with ending the employment relationship. Looking back, I can see that in my business dealings I was clear about my values and who I wanted in my room. I was thorough and firm.

Happy and grateful in the midst of my professional success, I couldn't understand why I was failing so miserably in my personal life.

Way before I heard the question "Who's in your room?" I fell in love with a man who I now recognize had very different values than I do. We had a whirlwind romance. There was something intoxicating about being close to him—he was charming and funny and wildly romantic. But something else about him began to emerge just after we moved in together, little clues that exposed a different side to him.

One day I was walking my dog when it started to rain. I turned around to head back home, and then my special squeeze pulled up in his sports car. Since we were both headed home, I asked if my dog and I could hop in with him. His "you've got to be kidding" look was the immediate answer. When I defaulted to defense and said I hadn't expected it to start raining, his look changed to one of disgust. He hated the idea that this not particularly large, damp, and possibly muddy dog would be riding in his fancy car. He hinted that I was being selfish and disrespectful by asking for a ride. In that moment, I didn't want to argue—I decoded his look. Besides, I felt foolish for having asked when I already knew what the answer would be. I told him I'd see him soon, and closed the door. He drove off. I walked home with wet cheeks—rain, tears, you call it. Clearly, we valued different things.

When I got home I wanted to talk with him about it. I wanted him to see that I had found the way he behaved very hurtful. In the midst of "wanting to talk about it," I suddenly realized that the kind of thing that had just happened was actually happening quite often. I tried to express how his actions affected me. He got angry, saying I was "beating him down" and trying to change him, when my goal had been simply to try to help him discover a more loving way to be. Our relationship became emotionally exhausting, full of highs and lows that eventually gave way to mostly lows. John Gray was definitely onto something when he wrote that "men are from Mars, women are from Venus." Finally, my partner moved out of my house when we decided there was no way we could make it work.

I felt conflicted about ending the relationship. On the one hand, I am an intelligent, successful young woman who knew this relationship was not working well. But I felt invested in it; I felt like I'd invested in him. It was so difficult to walk away from that emotional investment. I thought about how I value forgiveness and compassion, and felt that perhaps I should have been a better example of those qualities for him. I wanted the relationship to become healthy, to evolve, and for us to evolve together to become better people. I thought about all the things I could have done to make the relationship better. I wanted to take responsibility for my contributions and heal our hurt, but I couldn't get there from here. When I walked away, I felt that I was a horrible failure.

Time passed, and I began to realize that although walking away was one of the most emotionally challenging things I'd ever done, it was also the best thing I could have done for my own well being. But the difficulties of our relationship still affect me to this day because, as I now know, he lives on in my room.

After a two-year hiatus from men, I went out on a date that had been about eight months in the making. My date was the best friend of the man who bought my business, and for whom I now do consulting work. He put it this way, "My good friend has just gone through a separation. Natalie, he is the best man I know. I believe you two would have a lot in common. I would really love it if you guys met and, if nothing else, I think you could have a great friendship."

The timing seemed fortuitous, because I had just worked with the question of "Who's in your room?" I had come to appreciate and focus on my own values and the people who shared them. Perhaps before this I had unconsciously believed that living by these principles in my romantic relationships was, well, somehow unromantic!

This man and I went out for dinner and shared a lovely time. We ended up chatting for hours, closing the restaurant down. And it wasn't the flicker of candlelight, a memorable meal, or any Hollywood-style scene of someone playing a violin by the table that made me feel warm. I just found him to be a kind, goodhearted person, and had a really good feeling about him. Because of the timing, what I was looking for in the conversation was a values match -- the first time I had ever sat across the table from someone actively looking for a foundation for deep friendship that could allow love to emerge and flourish. I felt aware and mindful in this exploration, and it felt so right to be going about getting to know someone this way. Contrary to my earlier apprehensions, it did not seem unromantic at all. Actually, romance began to feel safe again.

The man sitting across from me that night was a businessman. His family owned a small airline that he and his brother ran. The airline had about 300 employees and a fleet of about 25 aircraft. One of the business values we shared was a dedication to employees having a great at-work experience. This truly matters in the service industry. We both believed that it is simply an ethical must to ensure that the workplace continually offers people an opportunity to transform and grow. We both loved the art of doing business well. I especially loved nurturing the spirit of entrepreneurship in others and myself.

So there I was, at 31 years old, for the first time in my personal life tuning into this process of focusing on mutual values. What on earth was I thinking, to never use these principles before in this aspect of my life? For me, in the past, dating had always been like stumbling around with a blindfold on, never using any of the tools I used so successfully in the business side of my life.

I find that living from clear values is often not easy. It's hard because it asks that I be always vigilant. It means that I am often implementing a closed-door policy to my room. In each moment it seems so much simpler to be lazy and say, "Do come in." I don't want people to think that I am not a nice person. In a way, this path is about choosing between instant gratification (short-term comfort with often negative long-term results) and trusting that if I choose carefully moment-by-moment, my life will become richer and more satisfying in the long run. It's very easy for us to sell out our personal values and opt for instant gratification. But if we keep doing this, we end up living shallow, unfulfilling lives.

I don't know what's going to happen with this new friendship—whether or not it may become the love of my life. What I have learned is that the moment I seek a values match, my life immediately begins to change for the better—immediately. It feels like a light switch has turned on. Going forward, I cannot imagine living any other way. Happily, I find that I'm able to forgive myself for the past, as I embrace what I had to go through to learn to be able to live differently today.

———————————

We were surprised to discover how many people thought that it was more romantic to leave this love aspect of their lives to random chance. When we asked them how this approach was working for them the answer was often, "not so much." When you apply the room concept to your life on a daily basis, you'll find that your values permeate every corner of your life and direct who you should let into your room. As a choreographer for your love life your doorman takes on some qualities of a guardian angel. All good.

Chapter 15

38 to Zero or Zero to 38?
A Tale of Two Rooms

You face choices in your life, as well as within the organizations that are part of your life. How you manage these choices can make all the difference.

Jeff's Story

> *Jeff Ensinger is the Executive Director of the Central Illinois Region of BNI. In the story below, Jeff vividly illustrates the need for a well-trained doorman when evaluating prospective members. His story is a tale of two chapters, with two dramatically different outcomes. One BNI chapter in his region went from zero to 38 people in a few months and was a great success; the other chapter went from 38 to zero, and they had a costly catastrophe on their hands.*

"Who's in your room?" I can't imagine a more powerful question. When it comes to BNI, I learned long ago to think carefully and listen to my gut when considering new members for our chapters, or when helping members in my region do the same for their chapters. You could say I learned some lessons the hard way, and my mistakes were harsh — but excellent — teachers.

These days, I like to meet new people as they approach BNI. When I meet these people, I find that either I feel good — you know that warm, fuzzy feeling?—or I feel like I need to take a shower. When I started out learning how to build a network, I was not so selective. In one case, the first time I met a particular guy it was a shower moment. I just didn't feel comfortable. But I realized that I'm not really in control of the selection process within each chapter. Plus, I knew that somebody was sponsoring him, and I figured that individual probably knew something I didn't know.

So I ignored my gut and let it go. Big mistake—big, big mistake!

The problems began with sporadic attendance. When the group leadership tried to talk to him about his poor attendance, he became angry and defensive. The other members felt a little intimidated and backed off, *and I let them.* That was my next big mistake.

Then other issues began to surface. Members were becoming aware of his poor job performance with clients. Again, they tried to confront him; again, he reacted angrily and defensively. And again, the leadership backed off.

Finally, a really big problem developed. On one particular project, his work was incomplete and poorly done, to say the least. The customer — a fellow network member — refused to pay. Both sides had started to take legal action against each other. At that point, the membership committee had had enough and finally booted the problem member out.

End of story? No. This man began to send harassing emails and make angry phone calls to a variety of individuals in the chapter, including me. Members began to quit. I even had to get my own attorney involved — at my own expense, of course. After a while, this man even went after my attorney, filing a complaint against him with the Illinois Bar Association. As a result, my attorney had to travel out of town to defend himself before the bar. He was exonerated of any wrongdoing, of course, but the whole process was time consuming and a terrible distraction from his work.

When all was said and done, more than 40 people suffered tremendous stress, the entire chapter was demolished, I was out a lot of money for attorney's fees, and my attorney had taken precious time away from his practice to clear his own name.

If only I had listened to my gut, my inner self, in the beginning. If only I had monitored the situation more closely, and advised the membership committee to look more carefully and move more slowly. If only I had urged the members to stand strong and remove the member much earlier, when things first began to turn sour.

As I said, my experience was a harsh teacher, and I learned my lesson well. Most importantly, I learned the best problem prevention is the *earliest* prevention. So I'd like you to think about it: Who are you about to let into your room?

My other story is a much happier one. Long ago, in a different year and different town, I had the great joy of stepping in to lead a new BNI chapter. When I took over the presidency we had six members. We had some really great officers who did their jobs well, but there were two non-officer members who came into the chapter and really lit our fire. We took off like a rocket.

These two individuals were outgoing types who knew everybody. They could walk into any building or event, walk up to anybody, and in a matter of minutes get to know that person. When we were preparing for a Visitor's Day, they went out and talked to everybody they knew. That day, we had 45 people in the room— even the mayor!

Eventually we grew to 38 members, and that chapter still exists today. I have to credit those two individuals for the way we grew and thrived—they were superstars. We owed our success mainly to them.

They were the kind of individuals who didn't mind giving with no guarantee of reward. They intuitively understood the philosophy of generosity behind our BNI motto, *Givers Gain*. They wanted to be part of something exciting, so they went out and made it happen. Of course, as we all could predict, they benefited as well in many ways. But they weren't worried about that when they first went out to spread the word.

We owe these two members a debt of gratitude. Not just because they helped a chapter grow, but because they set an example for all of us — what we could be like, who we could become.

That's a story that's really two stories, one good and one not so good. What will your future story be like? In what direction are you and your chapter heading? Zero to 38? Or 38 to zero?

Chapter 16
Excuse Me, I Must Be in the Wrong Room

At some point in their lives, almost everyone will have to deal with a toxic person who has made it into their room. But it's not only about who's in our room, it's also about who's room we are in. One woman in a particular BNI chapter told us that the best thing a certain member could do for the group was to "call in sick!" "When he calls in sick, we have a great meeting," she said. She added that this particular member was a "funsucker"—whenever he showed up, he sucked the fun right out of the room.

Sometimes we find that we have entered a toxic room. In this situation, you can be as kind as you want, but sooner or later what you value will clash with the way some people are. And since you can't change them, well...

LuAnn's Story

LuAnn Buechler, CMP, has a master's degree in hospitality administration from the University of Wisconsin—Stout. She is the coauthor of Exceptional Care for Your Valued Clients, a book on the power of positive word choice in the customer service experience.

I have always been known as a positive person. But it's taken me a long time to accept that some people just have no apparent ability to be positive. You know the type— people who are constantly complaining, looking for the negative and acting negatively. All they do is bring others down.

For many years, I just accepted that people in my life who were negative had to be tolerated. Worse yet, I spent many more years trying to change them to be more positive. Of course, we have no power to change anyone; they must find it within themselves to change. The best we can do is set an example.

Throughout my life, I found myself continually working in professional situations with these types of negative people. When this person was someone with authority, like a boss or manager, it was the absolute worst situation. But I always told myself, You just have to deal with it to keep the job. However, there was one situation that got so bad I had no choice but to leave a job I loved.

The two men that had been "let into my room" were brothers. One was the general manager of the hotel I worked at, and the other was the food and beverage director. I was the director of sales and catering. The two of them bickered constantly, like teenage girls, often working against each other instead of with each other, in what appeared to be a struggle over who was smarter. Unfortunately, I often found myself caught in the middle of their childish competition.

One evening, after the offices were closed to the public, I was working late and overhead the two of them get into a knockdown, drag-out screaming match. I have no recollection of the issue they were arguing over, but suddenly I knew I could no longer work in this toxic environment. It wasn't so much that I'd let them into my room—I'd let myself into theirs—which is really two sides of the same coin. Having been hired by the owner of the hotel, I went directly to him with my resignation and the reason for it. I had hoped that he would see the toxicity of the situation, and make a change in management for the good of the entire hotel staff.

That wasn't going to happen, however. In an attempt to keep me on the job "in their room," the owner wanted to pay me an additional salary -- over and above what I was being paid by the hotel—to stay and continue to put up with the situation. I had to refuse and excuse myself from their room.

Life's too short to live (or work) in a toxic environment. I felt I had no choice at that point but to leave a job I loved, and was well paid for, in order to remove myself from this daily barrage of negativity. The choice to leave in this case was a baby step in my learning curve toward removing this kind of negativity from my life.

Over and over again, my life choices and job selections led me into similar negative environments. I would tolerate the situation for a period of time, thinking that this was just the way life is, until I was unable to take it anymore and have to move on. I began to think that something was wrong with me; it seemed I was unable to commit to a job or employer, as I was moving on about every five years. There was a definite pattern. I've heard it said that some people tend to start their own businesses because they are otherwise unemployable. I may have been employable, but it never seemed to end well, so I started making other plans.

Shortly after starting my own business, through a blessed series of events and referrals, I attended certification training for the Passion Test Workshop. I went with my daughter Ashley, who was invited to become a facilitator of the program on the premise that it would be a great bonding experience for both of us to participate in the training. During that weekend, however, I discovered the people I really wanted to always be in my room.

After that training, I declared that going forward I would remove all the negative people from my life. Constant complainers beware—there is no room in my room for you. Now, I teach people how to eliminate the negative from their lives and look for the positive in every moment.

Life's too short to spend a lot of time in a room full of negativity. Excuse yourself from the rooms of negative people. Surround yourself with positive, supportive people. Fill your room with people you want to be like and live with. After all, you only have one room to work with; fill it wisely with only the positive things in life.

Sometimes you wake up in the wrong room and wished you hadn't spent the night. If you keep doing that, it's a sign that you have to wise up in the choices you're making. So get clear about your values (see Chapter 23), and train your doorman really well. Then have your doorman check out the values of the occupants of the rooms you are thinking of entering and be mindful before becoming a roommate.

Chapter 17
Doors Can Open in Unexpected Places

You don't always know who is going to end up being an enduring friend and colleague when you are selectively letting people into your room. But if your values are in line with theirs, chances are they can become assets to you in times of stress and change. Doors can open in the most unexpected places to offer you opportunity and fulfillment. When it comes to networking, you never know who knows someone who might be of value to you, and you never know what a particular contact can lead to.

Dorothy's Story

> *Dorothy Randall Saviste is a franchise owner and trainer for Referral Institute South West Florida. She helps entrepreneurs and small business owners grow their businesses through the power of word-of-mouth marketing. Dorothy has served as the BNI Area Director Consultant for Lee and Collier Counties (Florida) since 2009.*

After spending 15 years as a stay-at-home mom, finding a job—let alone a career—appeared to be nearly impossible. I was facing a divorce, my children were in their teens, and I had a degree in education but all my certificates had expired. My chances of finding a job with which I could support myself seemed pretty slim.

My first job opportunity came from two men I was serving on a Little League board with. They heard I was about to start looking for a job when they approached me and offered me a job at their bank as a safe deposit box attendant. I knew nothing about banking, but evidently I didn't have to. After nearly 2.5 years of working at the bank, serving in several capacities, I was promoted to operations supervisor of the main branch. Thank you, Ed Ramos and Nick Panicaro.

Speaking of that promotion: I was working in customer service, which I loved, when my supervisor invited me to lunch. She and I had become friends, but mostly we admired and respected each other. At lunch she mentioned that she had been given permission to hire an operations supervisor. She went on to say she was choosing me! I could not believe my ears. I had just been promoted over people who had been in banking for much longer than I had. They not only had more experience, but many were better connected in the community than I was. I actually said no at first!

She went on to explain that she knew banking; she didn't need me for that. She needed me to handle the disgruntled customers and tough employee issues. I love disgruntled customers and tough employee issues, so I took the job. Thank you, Leah Kirby.

In 2001 I did something I had not previously needed to do -- I actually interviewed for a job, this time in the title business. That interview wasn't as impactful as what happened next. In 2003 I was working as a closer at the title agency. A friend from the title company invited me to dinner. She told me that she was planning to open her own title company and wanted me to work for her. She was someone I liked and respected, so I immediately accepted the position.

She then asked, "Don't you want to know what you are going to do?" I thought this was a silly question -- I was a closer. She told me she wanted me to be her marketer. A marketer? I'm not a marketer, I protested. "Yes, you are," she said "you just don't know it." Once she told me what she was going to pay me to be a marketer, I remembered, "That's right, I am a marketer!" Thank you, Wendi Jamison.

As her marketer, I was introduced to BNI. I was a nervous wreck at my first BNI meeting, but I found the members of the chapter to be so friendly, helpful and warm that I fit right in. Occasionally a director would visit the chapter. I didn't know him well, but when it came time to choose a leadership team, he suggested I become the next president of the chapter. Are you kidding me? I was six months into this BNI thing and they were asking me to be president? Well, I was terrified, but took the position anyway. Now, that same Director Consultant and I hold the Area Director Consultant Position (and have since 2009). Thank you, Mark Stough.

Are these the five people I would have consciously chosen to be in my room—back then before I had a doorman? I am not sure, but the way they helped me shape my career (four jobs, no official interviews), increase my confidence and discover my talents are what made me chose them. Without their belief and faith in me, the confidence they instilled and the encouragement they gave, I would not be the person I am. They would be surprised of the impact they had on my life. What I have learned is the generosity and wisdom of the people in your room are very important to the quality of the life that you live.

Life is often a one-thing-leads-to-another kind of deal. Whether we like the deal or not has lot to do with our thoughtstyle. If we have developed a growth-oriented thoughtstyle, life is likely to be a serendipitous journey—in other words, it will look like we got lucky a lot of the time. Serendipity means a "happy accident" or "pleasant surprise" -- a fortunate mistake. Specifically, it means the accident of finding something good or useful while not specifically searching for it. We have interviewed a lot of very successful men and woman over the years that ascribe their success to serendipity. What we discovered is that these people in fact seem to have made their own luck as a consequence of a ferocious commitment to growth and discovery. This was their thoughtstyle. Make it yours.

Chapter 18
Some Lessons Cost More Than Others

What happens when you let the wrong person into your room? Even worse is what can happen when you realize your mistake, but the person has really wedged themselves in and will not leave. This can turn into a really painful experience, and, if you're in business, an extremely costly one.

Ivan's Story

Ivan Misner, PhD, is the founder and chairman of BNI, the world's largest business networking organization. He has written 19 books, including the New York Times bestseller Masters of Networking and the number-one bestseller Masters of Success. Ivan is a monthly columnist for entrepreneur.com and is chairman of the board of the Referral Institute, a referral training company that has trainers around the world.

A few years ago my company was in the midst of one of the largest projects in the history of our organization. The project was very complex and financially challenging, and involved many people. It was also in trouble.

I needed to select a key player to manage the project team. The man I chose was very qualified, with incredibly strong technical skills. He was the perfect person to help turn the project around—or so I thought.

I also knew that he came with a considerable amount of baggage. He didn't always play well with others. From time to time when talking to people he would fly off the handle emotionally, bringing an immense amount of drama to the workplace. But as I noted, he was highly qualified for the work.

I have lived most of my life as a highly rational guy. I can relate to Spock from *Star Trek*—though I don't have the pointed ears. Although my gut was sending out yellow alerts, I hired this person based on his qualifications. I suspected there would be problems with the drama and outbursts, but I believed I could coach him and guide him through it. I thought that if we had the emotional intelligence to handle ourselves we could reel in someone who lacked self-awareness, at least enough to stay on track and get a vital project completed on schedule.

It turns out I was wrong—monumentally wrong. Despite his incredible technical skills, this person's behavior more than offset his strengths. The project went from problematic to horrific within a year. It was way over budget, well behind schedule, and not nearly of the quality that I expected. One day, one of the team members told me that the best thing the project manager could do for a meeting was to call in sick! The team member said that when this manager was not around, they got a lot more done.

The problems weren't totally obvious at first glance. It wasn't like I would come into meetings with a clear agenda and get immediately derailed by a shouting match. The manager didn't leap about the room screaming, throwing things, or knocking over chairs like a Bobby Knight on steroids. With someone like that, you begin to suspect they have some kind of bipolar condition or other serious disorder. Or they become so disruptive that their actions are grounds for dismissal.

It was more just a case of bad chemistry, of this person not getting along with other people and not being a team player. Keep in mind that I really, really needed this person, and I had made a logical decision to put up with almost anything to get the project done. Ultimately I made a bad decision, but it took me a while to admit just how wrong I had been. I'd dealt with worse, I told myself… but maybe I hadn't. Maybe this was my new worst.

When I first came across the concept of "Who's in your room?" I decided right then and there that this project leader should never have been in my room. I understood that removing him from my room was going to be difficult and painful, but I knew that it had to be done. It ended up taking months to lay the groundwork, as I had to personally engage different team members with parts of the project they needed to know about but hadn't been privy to because of this manager's dysfunctional control issues. I had to drop many of my regular responsibilities and devote an immense amount of time to this process. I promoted some people and moved others around. Finally, when everything was lined up, I made the move and let the project leader go.

There was an immediate and palpable change in the project. Today, it has made incredible strides—it's becoming exactly the product that I was hoping for, and is something I am proud of as an entrepreneur.

The biggest lesson I learned through this very expensive and very stressful process was this: be very selective about who you let into your room. Don't allow someone in just because of their technical skills or other narrow qualifications. I want a work environment that is a "drama-free" zone; I now pick people for my organization *who I want in my room*. I try to select qualified people who fit an organizational culture of collaboration, people who share information and knowledge and don't bring to the process a soap opera style of behavior.

I also learned another lesson: I need to trust my gut. I hear that's called "head-heart balance." My doorman and I are working on it.

———

It's never too late to do a little room cleaning when you find you've made a mistake, especially once you've evaluated the costs of that decision. Cleaning frenzy and chaos from your room and your life can be a very calming thing. Keep in mind the room concept isn't just about saying "no." Sometimes, it's about saying the right "yes."

Chapter 19

Getting to "Yes"

In this book, we've been talking a lot about saying "no": how to say no, when to say no, and to whom. So let's look at the positive side of saying "no"—it leaves you space in your life, and in your room, to get to say (the right) "yes."

Stephen's Story

Stephen Josephs is an executive coach, author, and consultant who is particularly interested in the intersection between business performance, psychology, and mind/body disciplines. He has embraced a daily practice of mind-body disciplines for more than four decades, including tai chi, qigong, aikido, and meditation. Stephen is a wonderful humorist, excellent classical guitarist and a celebrant of the human spirit.

My doorman is a talent scout. He looks for individuals who want to approach challenges and opportunities in ways they haven't considered before. They need to be open to experiment with new ways of thinking and, perhaps more importantly, refine their capacity to pay attention. They're the ones I want to fill my room with.

When I coach these kind of leaders, they get the most out of what I uniquely offer and it brings out the best in both sides.

Utilizing the room and doorman concepts means that you are not selecting everyone who comes along and letting them into your room. This is not so much about saying "no" to some people as it is about saying "yes" to the right people.

That's why I invest a great deal of time vetting potential coaching clients. I offer risk-free initial sessions so I can come to deeply understand them. Anyone who visits my website can fill out a form requesting one of these sessions, but I don't automatically accept everyone. This care and attention has been the secret of my success and happiness in my work. When I look at my calendar and see the names of clients I am scheduled to talk to, I look forward to every one of those conversations. To me, that's heaven. These are the people I have mindfully said "yes" to.

I don't worry about refusing people. Sometimes it can be just the right thing. Think of it this way. Saying "no" to some people leaves you space in your room to open the door to saying "yes" to other people—the right "yes."

Whether he's scouting talent or choosing who gets in your room, a good doorman benefits everyone. When we let him do his job, we end up living in a place that is truly our home.

―――――――――――――

Your room is your home, and should feel as good as your favorite chair. Sometimes the comfort you get from the room also has a lot to do with the person who inspired you, by giving you the template you used to create your room.

Chapter 20
Your Room Should Feel Like Home to You

When someone finds out a room is to be theirs, right away you see them getting a few throw pillows, putting up pictures, or maybe changing the curtains. It's part of ownership. It's your room—why shouldn't it reflect the influences that make you, well, you?

Patricia's Story

Patricia Lanza is the mother of seven children, grandmother of nine, and an author and lecturer. After her children were grown and gone, and after her life as a Navy wife and innkeeper was over, she reinvented herself as a single grandmother, full-time gardener and writer. She created her new life with a method she calls Lasagna Gardening. Legendary publisher Rodale Press took notice and signed a contract for Lasagna Gardening: No Digging, No Tilling, No Weeding, No Kidding!, *which appeared in 1998.*

Pat went on to publish Lasagna Gardening for Small Spaces *in 2002 and* Lasagna Gardening with Herbs *in 2004. She says that its all began with the time she spent in her grandmother's room as a very young child.*

When I was a child, growing up in the Cumberland Mountains of eastern Tennessee, I would watch my widowed grandmother get ready to plant a garden. She would hitch the mule to an old plow and, throwing the reins over her shoulders, guide the plow up and down, making long straight rows. Grandmother was a small woman; the mule was big and the plow heavy. The soil was one part dirt and two parts rock. I can't imagine how hard it was to plant that garden --watching her do it made a lasting impression on me. It was there that the seed was sown that would one day grow into a gardener.

I tagged along beside my grandmother for the much of the first years of my life. I learned to count by dropping seeds in furrows. As grandmother prepared a hill for potatoes and squash, I came behind and carefully placed the seed potatoes or the right number of squash seeds. She would trust me to place a dipper of water into each hole where a tomato or cabbage plant was dropped. When planting was finished, she would bring out a Mason jar of dried flower seeds and, in two feet of space around the perimeter of the garden, sprinkle them on top of the ground. She would use a lawn rake to mix up the soil a bit, then flatten the surface of the soil with the end of the rake.

By the height of the season, my grandmother's garden

was a beautiful sight. The rows of vegetables, in various stages of growth and ripening, were surrounded by the brightly colored, mixed annuals. When friends or family came to visit, she would send them home with a wonderful country bouquet wrapped with a few sheets of wet newspaper covering the cut ends. The family saw the best of the blossoms in Mason jars on the kitchen table at supper time.

When the flowers were finished for the season, my grandmother would pull the bottom ends of her apron up in one hand, making it into a carrying cloth, and walk along the outside edge of the garden. With her free hand, she pulled off the dried flower seeds and dropped them into her apron. She kept them in paper bags until she was sure they were dry; then she would store them in Mason jars for the next season. Each year she would add to her flower mixture by gathering seeds from her fellow gardeners.

During the summer, grandmother hoed weeds and carried water to keep her garden growing in the intense Tennessee heat. She would let me help pick bugs from potatoes and beetles from beans. I would drop seed corn into rows and hill up squash and melon mounds. I carried garden and kitchen waste to the compost pile long before I ever heard the word compost. As fall came around, grandmother stepped up the pace, for everything she grew had to be canned, dried, and preserved. I still find it unbelievable that one little grandmother could have done so much.

When I look back at the time I spent with my grandmother, I can't remember her talking very much, but each time she did I would pay attention. Watching and listening to my grandmother as she grew and preserved our food and medicines inspired me. Seeing a garden planted with a border of flowers each year gave me a longing for beauty. All of it seeped into my very being. She trained me to be a gardener and a hard worker without ever verbalizing her intent. Everything I learned from her makes me the gardener I am today.

I took all the knowledge I gleaned from this uneducated but wonderfully intelligent woman with me when I left the mountains. It came in handy when I married a man who was in the military and we had to move every three years. I used that knowledge to help raise my family of seven children, run my home, and become a good gardener. I was always able to grow some of our food, find other food in the wild, and then preserve, can, and freeze that food. I kept my children near me in the garden where we planted, worked, and weeded together.

With each move we started a new garden, and we learned

what grew best in each area. With our last move, to New York State, we became innkeepers with little time for gardening. Our inn had only nine rooms but featured 250 seats for food service. At first I had only an herb garden by the kitchen door, where we could pick fresh chives, dill, basil, and parsley. Later I expanded the herb garden to grow enough herbs to dry and save, including oregano, tarragon, anise, and many others. My family and I learned the joys of picking and eating wild blueberries and growing rhubarb that we could harvest for the entire season. Gardening in the short, cool summers of the Catskill Mountains was a challenge for most vegetables, but the freezer was full of blueberries, raspberries, blackberries, currants, and chopped rhubarb.

As my children grew up and left home, gardening became a solitary pleasure. I soon found that traditional gardening—all that tilling, digging, hoeing, and weeding—was too much work. I began to search for easier ways to do all that was needed to have my vegetable, herb, and flower gardens. Memories of my grandmother returned. All I had learned so many years ago came back to me as I worked alone. But what I needed to do was adapt those lessons I learned to a new way of gardening: a way to have the best soil with the least effort. *Lasagna Gardening* was my answer.

We'd like you to contemplate something important that Pat's story illustrates: You don't have to construct the idea for your room from scratch. The template of your room, like hers, can be one you inherit—a legacy room, if you will—where you feel an instant comfort. Pat's grandmother created the template for that place where Pat could feel right and true about who and what she let into her room. What a kind gift for anyone to pass on to future generations!

Chapter 21

Building a Room

Change is part of life, and you won't always have the same configuration to your room. How you adjust it is up to you – the change can be positive, or not so much. The transformation possibilities are there, however, for you to rise like the Phoenix from the ashes to a far better place.

BNI is all about people's experience. They are going to come to the meetings and either have a good experience or a bad experience, which will be determined by the way the group is run and the results they receive. You can have a massive influence on their experience as well as your own.

The basic metaphor of "Who's in your room?" is about your room. You will meet people along the way who will help you build it. Sometimes you visit their rooms. Sometimes it's just a few degrees of separation that heralds serendipity, and we discover that we make our own luck, as the legend of the Princes of Serendip suggests.

Beth's Story

Beth Sobiloff founded Birchwood Web Design in 2002. The company serves mostly small business owners on the South Shore, Boston and Cape Cod areas of Massachusetts, but it has customers across the globe. Beth is an Assistant Director with the BNI chapter of Southeastern Massachusetts and Rhode Island.

They say that everyone comes into your life for a reason. Sometimes you let them into your room because they appear to be someone who would be very good for you, someone who complements your traits and makes you happy.

But then, things change.

This was the case when I met my now ex-husband. He was handsome, witty, intelligent—and a musician. I've always had a weakness for musicians! We started dating. Life was great. I fell in love with him.

It wasn't long before his hot temper became apparent. He never hit me, but his words stung just as badly. His criticism eroded my already fragile self-esteem, until I felt worthless. But no sooner would the harsh words be out of his mouth then he would be apologizing for the things he said, buying me flowers, and putting me back up on a pedestal. Yes, the classic cycle of abuse, you might say. So why didn't I leave his room? For many of us, it's not all that easy -- when you're in the middle of it, it can be hard to see the forest for the trees.

Eventually, I did get out of his room. Actually, he left me, but I take credit for it. Why? Because when I started standing up for myself, he started backing away. That change probably never would have happened had I not allowed someone else into my room—a counselor.

I joined this counselor's self-esteem group. All eight women in the group had people in their rooms that were holding them back, making them feel unworthy and undeserving. The counselor didn't tell us to get up and leave the room of our abusers. In some cases, the abuser was a mother or father. Instead, she taught us how to embrace the goodness in them, hold the child that was within them close to us, and realize that they were doing the best they knew how.

It was then that I realized that my lack of self-esteem was my own doing. I was allowing myself to feel stupid, selfish, and ugly. That realization changed everything. From then on, I could deal with the fact that my ex-husband was in my room permanently, but I had chosen to not allow him to control my destiny. And that was not easy, because he tried to use our son to manipulate both of our lives. That was very hard to watch. My son idolized his father and feared him at the same time. By staying strong and providing a stable environment for my children (I had two others from a previous marriage, whom he had adopted), we all got through it. I think my children are stronger people as a result.

Fast forward 10 years, and I found myself getting laid off from my job. I had seen it coming and had decided to take a Webmaster certificate course in preparation for a career change. After I finished the course, I was hired by a company as their in-house Webmaster. Things were great for a while, and then 9/11 happened. Many of the company's projects were put on hold, and my job was eliminated. No one was hiring Web designers, so I was left with no choice but to start my own business.

Had I not been through the experiences I'd had with my ex-husband, I'm not sure I ever would have had the nerve to take this giant step. The next room that I entered would also prove to be life changing.

It was a BNI room.

Someone from my previous company suggested that I join BNI as a way to grow my business with referrals. The closest chapter to my home was a 25-minute ride away, but that did not deter me. I showed up at the meeting and was immediately embraced. Many of the business owners in the room already knew that they needed to have a website, even though it was still a concept that was not universally accepted. I received two referrals at that first meeting and never looked back. My new business and my attitude toward life were changed forever.

From the *"Givers Gain"* philosophy to the camaraderie of a room full of entrepreneurs, I thrived in what was the beginning of a lifelong journey of learning, giving, and receiving. I had never done any business networking at all, so I got to learn the right way to create relationships with others, to build their trust in me and mine in them.

I started building my room like I never had before. I was making conscious decisions about who was being invited in and who was not. I surrounded myself with like-minded men and women who were working hard to grow their businesses, and who were as interested in helping me grow mine as they were in growing their own.

That doesn't mean that everything was perfect or easy! Being in business for oneself is fraught with trials and tribulations. Building relationships is not the fastest way to get customers, but it is the best way, in my opinion. Once someone is in my room, getting to know them, finding out what they're all about, and asking how I can help them enriched my own life. Even if they don't show the same interest in me in the beginning, I make it my primary concern to find out how I can help them.

I became very involved in networking activities, eventually becoming the president of a local Chamber of Commerce, serving on the board of directors of a women's networking group, and taking various leadership positions in BNI. I was always most concerned with how I could help others.

In return, I have forged lifelong relationships with people who will always be in my room. Many of them have helped me build my business as well. They have become loyal clients and have recommended me to the people in their rooms. I still get referrals from people I let into my room many years ago, even if we haven't remained in close contact.

This has taught me another valuable lesson. It's really true that once you let someone in your room, they are in your room forever. So don't take them for granted; nourish your relationships. If you regret letting someone into your room, knowing that they will in some way affect your life forever, get the best that you can from that relationship. Take lemons and make lemonade, as they say.

When people open their room to you it can change the course of your life, even when the time you spend in their room is not long. Sometimes the time we spend can feel like a deep learning experience. We continue this idea in the next chapter.

Chapter 22
You Shape Your Room, and Somtimes A Room Shapes You

Not only are there people and projects in your room, but you are in other people's rooms, by yourself or as part of a project. This means that the values and influence involved are also a two-way exchange. This can be a good thing or a bad thing, depending on whether your values-driven doorman was vigilant about who and what got let in, as well as where you and your projects were allowed to go out.

Syd's Story

Syd Field has been acclaimed as the "guru of all screenwriters" by CNN and "the most sought-after screenwriting teacher in the world" by the Hollywood Reporter. An internationally celebrated author of eight books on screenwriting, his book Screenplay is considered "the Bible" of the film industry -- published in some 28 languages and used in more than 450 major colleges and universities around the country. He has conducted screenwriting workshops all over the world and been a special script consultant to the governments of Argentina, Australia, Austria, Brazil, Germany, Israel, Mexico, and more. Syd was inducted into the prestigious Final Draft Hall of Fame in 2006.

When I was still a young kid, a documentary film producer at Wolper, doing research for five years, I learned that I could find stuff. That was my gift—I could find stuff. I found the actual Bay of Pigs footage that was shot on the boat as they were traveling to invade Cuba. I found Grace Kelly's first modeling spread, shot when she was 17 years old and still in high school. I found the first film clip Marilyn Monroe ever made—a Union 76 commercial. She went by her birth name of Norma Jean Baker at that time.

I was learning that I could find things *if I set my mind to it.* I became aware that, with this change in mental strategy and energy, I could put that energy out into the world and opportunities would start to find me. I could then make different choices about who I wanted to be as a person and what I wanted to do. I remember the "A ha!" moment when I recognized that I could make the choice to be in a room of a success or nonsuccess. That literally changed my life. In that moment, I realized that I could choose the life I wanted.

This was also when I had the opportunity to write my first book and to start teaching. This was back in the 1970s, times of great exploration and experimentation. I was fortunate to be within the crucible of that time of great change in the film industry. We were all setting out along this unknown path of experimentation, in making television the way we wanted to see television. You can't do that now, of course, but that's how we started, going around to show what could be done and creating what we called entertainment documentaries, the forerunner of shows like *Law and Order.*

When I started out teaching, I was terrible. I was the worst you can imagine, because I felt that if I'm hired to be the teacher and you guys are the students, I have to know something that you don't. It made me the worst teacher; students were leaving in droves every night. Nobody wanted to be in my room.

At least I could figure out it wasn't working. So I thought, "Why don't I turn the room upside down? I'll be a student and they'll be the teacher." I opened up the class to questions from the students. I answered from my own experience as a reader, writer, and now a teacher. I began to realize that everybody has the same questions regarding how to write a screenplay.

How do you tell your story? How do you structure a

story? How do you create the characters, write more effective dialogue, and shape strong and complex characters? This became the structure for the book. I read a lot of screenplays along the way—at least 10–15,000, and probably 20,000 by now. I've sold screenplays, had a few produced, and had quite a few optioned. As I'm looking back, I see that there were certain signposts that directed me as I was moving along this path. I didn't even know that teaching was one of them until I found out that I could take questions from people and not be an ass in front of the class or assume I knew something they didn't. I went back to writing and finally sat down to put together chapter outlines for a book. I wrote an introduction and then two chapters, and got it sold within two weeks. I've been writing and teaching all over the world ever since.

Now the whole film industry is being reinvented. The power of the big studios and the mainstream media is vanishing, just like the world changed in the music industry. All of us in the business of film and television have to reinvent our identities and roles.

What's interesting to me is the growth I'm going through right now. At this moment in time, and after all these years, I'm still not totally clear about who I am, because I'm changing with the current of the times—

reinventing my role as I am carried along by the current. The self, to me, is a conscious thing, and any conscious thing lives, grows, changes, and adapts to the times. If you don't adapt, it's over. You see that all the time. People who can't adapt get locked in nonsuccess until they perish.

Sam Peckinpah used to write about people who were unable to adapt to the present time. Sam invited me into his room and became a wonderful mentor to me. He believed that there were unchanged men in changing times, so he made *The Wild Bunch*, the story of four outlaws who are out of time. In a similar vein, you have the film *Butch Cassidy and the Sundance Kid*. The characters go to Bolivia because they can't adapt to the times of the railroad, the telephone, the check -- they're out of business, because all they know how to do is rob banks. In *The Wild Bunch*, it's the same way—all the characters know how to do is rob banks. Their trade, their identity, is as a bank robber. By 1907, however, things had changed, and they didn't know how to adapt to the change. So this idea about unchanged men in changing times is really important, and that's exactly what I'm beginning to understand.

I think about this "Who's in your room?" idea in an expanded way. I realize that the rooms I've been in have shaped my life in profound ways. It's not just about "Who's in my room?"—it's also about the rooms I enter.

You come and you go. People enter your room and you enter theirs. While in the rooms of your mentors and colleague— just as with your friends, family, and companions—you exchange what matters to you with them. The imprint of their influence goes on with you, and yours with them. As far as we know for sure, this is the one and only life we will be given. The question of who's in our room and the doorman principle can allow us to regard each breath we have left as sacred.

Chapter 23

How Will You Treasure the Breaths You Have Left?

You have no doubt thought about living a whole and complete life, and that is part of the intended benefit from applying the room concept. But have you thought much about your own death?

We want you to meet someone who confesses to becoming obsessed about death, who studied Buddhism, travelled to India, and visited gravesites but in the end found her values far closer to home, in her own room. Along with the question of "Who's in your room?" and the doorman principle, this idea of how you invest the breaths you have left can be truly life changing.

Geneen's Story

Geneen Roth is the author of eight books, including the New York Times bestsellers When Food Is Love, The Craggy Hole in My Heart and the Cat Who Fixed It, Women Food and God *and* Lost and Found. *She has been teaching groundbreaking workshops and retreats for over 30 years. Roth is a contributor to many publications, from* The Huffington Post *and*

Good Housekeeping *to* O:The Oprah Magazine, *and has appeared on numerous national shows, including* Oprah, 20/20, Good Morning America, The View *and* NPR's Talk of the Nation. *She lives in northern California with her husband.*

I learned so much from spiritual practice—about ease and loveliness and my crazy mind—but it didn't dispel my fears of death. If anything, it exacerbated them because I became more aware of the shortness of any life. My life, in particular. The old saying in Buddhist circles is that this human life is so precious that it is as if each one of us is like a turtle who lives in the ocean and comes up for air every hundred years. If by chance the turtle—aka you— puts her head through a bucket that is floating on the surface it would be extremely rare. Attaining a precious human life is even rarer than that. So, since you have a chance this one precious life to discover who you really are—your true nature—don't waste a single second.

Talk about pressure.

As I headed into my forties and fifties, people around me were dying or had died. My father, my dear friend Lew, my cat. My aunt Bea. My friend Linda. And every time, it was the same: how could a person (even those with four legs) be here one day and gone the next? Death was so irreversible, so final, so forever—unlike, say, buying a pair of shoes from Zappo's, changing your mind about their color, and being given a 365-day-free return policy.

But then, something unexpected happened: As part of a routine medical procedure, my throat closed, my heart rate skyrocketed, my blood pressure dropped and I had the strange sensation of leaving my body. I was conscious enough to realize that this was "It." I was dying. I remember being surprised that it was happening so quickly, and on an ordinary day in September. (I was hoping for harps and orchids and long soulful glances of loved ones when I died, not a cold tinny examination room with a nurse with a purple happy face pinned on her smock and a doctor with a wandering eye.)

Although there were many compelling insights during (and after) that near death experience, one that has remained with me is the visceral understanding that all my years of being death-obsessed weren't actually about dying or death; they were about life. They weren't about fear of the end, they were about longing to be awake in the middle. In what I called my life. I didn't want to get to the end and realize I hadn't actually been here. I wanted, as the poet Mary Oliver says, to have spent my life "married to amazement," not wedded to regret or exhaustion.

But after the medical procedure, I realized that death—those spiritual teachers weren't kidding—could happen to me on any ol' day. I realized this life I had wasn't a dress rehearsal for some bigger better promise of glory or happiness that was around the corner. This was it—it was all I had—and my breaths were numbered. I didn't how many breaths I had left, but it became apparent that no matter how charming I was or how many organic pomegranates I ate, not dying was not an option.

Within a few days of being home from the hospital, I made a list what I loved. Of what knocked on the door of my heart. Of what I would regret not doing if I had died in that examination room. The list was very short and incredibly simple. It included writing, being with my husband, spending time in nature, working with my students and being with my friends. It also included not rushing, meeting the eyes of the cashier at the grocery store/gas station/coffee shop, taking time every day to be still, being present with any task, even washing the dishes.

I began quitting things I didn't want to participate in. I said no to parties I didn't want to go to, invitations I didn't want to accept. I quit a graduate program in which I was enrolled, I started working on a book I'd wanted to write for years. I spent time with trees, particularly a maple tree in our driveway. I told my husband regularly what I cherished about him and our life together. Over and over, with each day and each choice, I asked myself: is this something on which I want to spend the breaths I have left? When you realize your breaths are numbered, your choices about what to do with the ones you have left become radically clear.

Five years have passed and I am still asking the breath question. Not always, of course. Sometimes when my husband and I are fighting, revenge, not breaths are uppermost in my mind. But even then, I can often pull myself back from the brink and remember that, really, we are all alive for about ten minutes and I don't want to miss a moment. Or a breath.

In a complex world—one that rushes at you at times like snowflakes at your windshield—simpler and valued is often quite a good thing. Another way to look at who and what you let into your room has to do with their cost in terms of the breaths you have left.

This would be a really good time to start working on your values clarification process in the next chapter.

Chapter 24

What Are Your Values?

As you explore each of the steps below, you should complete the relevant exercises. It helps to have a piece of paper and pen handy, or be at your computer to create a file. It would also be valuable to have most, if not all, of the members of your BNI group also assess their values, to gain insight on the focus of the entire chapter. Being in alignment on values as a group will make for a more successful room, and therefore a more successful chapter.

What Are Your Values?

Before you answer this question you need to know what, in general, values are defined as. Personal values are the standards that you set for yourself to live by.

Your values are the qualities that you believe are important in the way you live and work. They are invoked to determine your priorities, and, deep down, they're probably the standards you use to tell if your life is turning out the way you want it to or not. When the things that you do and the way you behave match your values, life is usually good—you feel satisfied and content. But when your actions do not align with your values, you will experience dissonance: the inner discord of your life being out of tune. This can lead to lingering unhappiness and depression.

This is why making a conscious effort to identify your values is so important. Life gets much better when you acknowledge your values—and when you make plans and decisions that honor them. Your values are not your values unless you live them. For example, if you value family, but success in a new job you are considering would require you to work 70-hour weeks and keep you from your family, you will feel internal stress and conflict—and you will ultimately fail. In this situation, a well-trained doorman will not let that job into your room.

When considering new opportunities, understanding your values enables you to choose wisely. When you know your own values, you can use them as guides in making decisions about how to live your life, and you can answer questions like these:

- What career should I pursue?

- Should I accept this promotion?

- Should I start my own business?

- Should I compromise, or be firm with my position?

- Should I follow family tradition, or travel down a new path?

- Should I begin a relationship with this person I am attracted to?

- Should I move forward in my current relationship?

So take the time to understand the real priorities in your life, and you'll be able to determine the best direction for you and your life goals.

Core values are usually fairly stable. As you move through life, however, your values may evolve. For example, when you first start your career, success— measured by money and status—might be a top priority. But after you have a family, work-life balance may be what you value more, and your personal definition of success begins to change to reflect your evolving values. This is why keeping in touch with your values is a lifelong exercise. You should continuously revisit your list of values, especially if you start to feel unbalanced and can't quite figure out why.

Defining Your Values

A good way to start out is to look back on your life and identify when you felt really good about things, confident that you were making good choices. As you go through the exercise below, be aware that values that were important to you in the past may not be as relevant now.

Step 1: Identify the times when you were happiest.

Find examples from both your career and personal life; this will ensure some balance in your answers. Then ask yourself:

- What were you doing?

- Were you with other people? Who?

- What other factors contributed to your happiness?

Step 2: Identify the times when you felt a sense of pride.

Use examples from your career and personal life. Ask yourself:

- Why were you proud?

- Did other people share your pride? Who?

- What other factors contributed to your feelings of pride?

Step 3: Identify the times when you were most fulfilled and satisfied.

Again, use both work and personal examples. Ask yourself:

- What need or desire was fulfilled?

- How and why did the experience give your life meaning?

- What other factors contributed to your feelings of fulfillment?

- Why is each experience truly important and memorable?

Step 4: Determine your top values, based on your past experiences of happiness, pride, and fulfillment.

As previously mentioned, all well curated rooms are governed by a set of values. You might draw up different lists of values for different purposes, such as having a list for your family life, your work life, your health life, your romantic life, and so on. But the overall exercise is driven by one common purpose: to help you to recognize, acknowledge, and establish a defined set of values by which you live.

As you'll soon see, every value must be objective and explicit. Use the following list of common personal values to help you get started. Aim for about 10 top values. (As you work through, you may find that some of the values naturally combine. For instance, if you value philanthropy, community, and generosity, you might say that service to others is one of your top values.)

First, look through the sample list of values. This will help you to get a sense of the values language, and the types of trigger words and adjectives you'll want to use in creating your own personal list. Mark or write down any word that triggers a recognition of something extremely important to you in your life. Aim to pick about 20 words from the list below that have meaning to you and that reflect strongly the person you want to be. It's natural to want to choose dozens of these words, but narrow it down to 20 or less. Read through the entire list first, think about them, and then re-read it with the aim of making your selections. Feel free to add words if you need to. Note that there is no explicit definition to any of these words or terms—you can define them however you want. The goal is simply for you to identify the terms that ring as important and true to you and your life.

Who's in Your Room?
The Quality of Your Life Depends on the People in Your Life

☐ Achievement/Drive	☐ Certainty
☐ Adaptability	☐ Challenging Problems
☑ Adding Value	☐ Change/Variety
☐ Advancement/Promotion	☐ Charisma
☐ Adventure	☐ Charity
☐ Aesthetic	☐ Cheerfulness
☐ Affection	☐ Chivalry
☐ Affinity	☑ Clarity
☐ Aliveness	☐ Close Relationships
☐ Articulateness	☐ Coaching
☐ Arts	☐ Commitment
☐ Attractiveness	☑ Communication
☐ Authenticity	☐ Community
☐ Awareness	☐ Companionship
☐ Beauty	☐ Compassion
☐ Bliss	☑ Competence
☐ Caring	☐ Competition

☐ Confidence

☐ Congruence

☐ Connection

☐ Conscientiousness

☐ Considerate

☐ Contribution

☑ Conviction

☐ Cooperation

☐ Courage

☐ Courteousness

☐ Creativity

☐ Decisiveness

☐ Democracy

☐ Dependability

☑ Discernment

☐ Discovery

☐ Ecological Awareness

☐ Economic Security

☑ Effectiveness

☑ Efficiency

☐ Empathy

☐ Endurance

☐ Energy

☐ Enthusiasm

☐ Environment

☐ Equality

☐ Ethical Practice

☐ Excellence

☐ Excitement

☐ Expertise

☐ Expression

☐ Fairness

☐ Fame

☐ Family

- ☐ Fast Living
- ☐ Fast-Paced Work
- ☑ Financial Gain
- ☐ Flexibility
- ☐ Focus
- ☑ Forgiveness
- ☐ Freedom
- ☐ Friendship
- ☐ Fun
- ☐ Giving
- ☐ Gratitude
- ☐ Growth
- ☑ God
- ☐ Happiness
- ☐ Having a Family
- ☑ Health
- ☐ Heart

- ☐ Helping Other People
- ☐ Helping Society
- ☐ Honesty
- ☐ Honor
- ☐ Humility
- ☐ Humor
- ☐ Inclusiveness
- ☐ Independence
- ☐ Influencing Others
- ☐ Inner Harmony
- ☐ Inspiration
- ☐ Integrity
- ☐ Intellectual Status
- ☐ Intelligence
- ☐ Intention
- ☐ Intimacy
- ☐ Involvement

Who's in Your Room?
The Quality of Your Life Depends on the People in Your Life

☐ Job Tranquility	☐ Merit
☐ Joy	☐ Money/Making Money
☐ Justice	☐ Music
☐ Kindness	☐ Nature
☐ Knowledge	☐ Nurturing
☑ Leadership	☐ Open and Honest
☐ Learning	☐ Openness
☑ Leverage	☐ Order
☐ Life	☐ Partnership
☐ Location	☑ Passion
☐ Love	☐ Patience
☐ Loyalty	☐ Peace
☐ Making a difference	☐ Perception
☐ Market Position	☐ Perseverance
☐ Meaningful Work	☑ Personal Growth
☐ Meditation	☑ Physical Challenge
☐ Mentorship	☐ Playfulness

Who's in Your Room?

The Quality of Your Life Depends on the People in Your Life

☐ Pleasure	☐ Resolution
☐ Power and Authority	☐ Resolve
☐ Presence	☐ Resourcefulness
☐ Privacy	☑ Respect
☐ Probability	☐ Responsibility
☑ Productivity	☐ Security
☐ Public Service	☐ Self-determinism
☐ Purity	☐ Self-Respect
☐ Purpose	☐ Sensitivity
☐ Quality	☐ Sensuality
☑ Quality Relationships	☐ Serenity
☐ Rational	☐ Sharing
☐ Receptivity	☐ Simplicity
☐ Recognition	☐ Sophistication
☐ Reliability	☐ Soul
☐ Religion	☐ Spirit
☐ Reputation	☑ Spiritual

☐ Spontaneity   ☐ Value

☐ Stability   ☐ Vigor

☐ Strength   ☐ Vision

☐ Status   ☐ Vitality

☐ Success   ☐ Vulnerability

☐ Supervising Others   ☐ Wealth

☐ Synergy   ☑ Wisdom

☑ Team/Teamwork   ☐ _____

☐ Technology   ☐ _____

☐ Tenderness   ☐ _____

☑ Time Freedom   ☐ _____

☐ Togetherness   ☐ _____

☐ Travel   ☐ _____

☑ Trust   ☐ _____

☐ Trustworthiness   ☐ _____

☐ Truth   ☐ _____

☐ Unity   ☐ _____

Now, on a separate piece of paper or document, choose 7 to 11 values that best define who you are. Add a sentence or two for each one describing how this value is important to you and how you express this value through your behavior. This is a really important step. It is often the case that people share the same value but live or express it differently. Sometimes these differences are a reflection of cultural norms. Behaviors that are considered respectful and loving in one culture might offend in another.

It's helpful to think of the different areas of your life where your values come into play. You may, for instance, want to create separate lists for "professional values," "parenting values," "social life values," "family values," and "financial values." There really is no hard and fast set of rules to follow here. The goal is to make this process as simple and straightforward as possible. Of course, if you break down your values into categories you will probably have some overlap, but you'll likely see patterns in your selections as you gravitate toward a set of standard values to live by.

A few words of warning may be in order here. It can be tempting to select and write down what you think your values should be, while being somewhat hazy about what they actually are. If you do this, it will create conflict for you down the road.

An excellent way to avoid this trap is to think of the five people you most like spending time with. Take five sheets of paper and put each of their names on the top of a sheet (you will find sample values sheets on our website). Next, select seven values that best describe each friend's core values. Then review the five sheets and look for the most commonly identified values, and write them down. The goal here is to end up with a list of the top seven most common values. You are now looking at your own core values.

If your list of current values does not reflect who you want to be, then it's time to get busy and train your doorman to help you make changes. You are going to need new friends—people who live in alignment with your values. You may even need a completely new set of friends and colleagues. This may sound harsh, but it's not. It is simply one of life's most important lessons.

Here is a sample list of possible personal values for you to use as a guide in completing this part of the exercise:

My Personal Values Are...

- **Family:** My family is my personal foundation. I cherish my time with my spouse and family and look for opportunities to grow with them.

- **Powerful Relationships and Teamwork:** I seek opportunities to grow and nurture strong, loving relationships with quality individuals. I know I will get further when I foster teamwork.

- **Leadership, Mentoring, and Coaching:** Leadership is the most important attribute of success. I seek like-minded mentors, colleagues, and employees. I enjoy both opportunities to mentor and coach others as well as being mentored and coached myself.

- **Achieving Big Things and Solving Complex Problems:** I look to achieve very large goals. I continually refine my ability to solve complex problems.

- **Physical and Spiritual Well-Being:** I maintain healthy practices, including diet, exercise, meditation, and the avoidance of things that may damage my health.

- **Adding Value:** I enjoy adding value wherever I can by helping things produce more and run more efficiently, from businesses to non-profits to families.

In some instances, it helps to also have a **Personal Declaration.** This is a more comprehensive document that details your values within a much richer context. It's broken down into sections, some of which are further divided to address the five main areas in most people's lives: 1) business/career, 2) financial, 3) family, 4) physical, and 5) spiritual. The Personal Declaration has room to explain your purpose in life, who you are in a single word, what your formula for success has been, what your legacy will be, what your long-term intentions are in those five areas, what your goals are given those intentions, and any affirmations or quotes that you like to use for motivation and inspiration.

We've included some sample Declarations to get you started. Note that you needn't create an entire Declaration in a day. This can be a document that you work on over the course of the next several weeks or months. For some people creating a simple list of values is plenty of work, and that exercise alone can take considerable time, thought, and effort. Be patient with yourself as you do these exercises. They are not meant to be completed in a single sitting.

Once you are comfortable with your list of values, it's time to move on.

Sample List of Values and Personal Declaration:

1. **Simplicity:** I enjoy keeping all aspects of my life as simple as possible. I avoid extravagance. I avoid "toys" and demonstrations of wealth. I enjoy keeping finances simple, debts low, and my life very simple.

2. **Family:** My family is my personal foundation. I cherish my time with my wife and family and look for opportunities to grow with them.

3. **Personal Growth:** Pursuing opportunities to increase my knowledge in all areas is a primary motivator for me. I realize that all progress starts with the pursuit of knowledge.

4. **Powerful Relationships and Teamwork:** I seek opportunities to grow and nurture strong, loving relationships with quality individuals. I know I will get further when I foster teamwork.

5. **Money—Making It and Giving It:** I enjoy making money and investing it. I aim to maximize profit in my business endeavors. I also enjoy using money for charitable purposes.

6. **Leadership, Mentoring, and Coaching:** Leadership is the most important attribute of success. I seek like-minded mentors, colleagues, and employees. I enjoy both opportunities to mentor and coach others, as well as being mentored and coached myself.

7. **Endurance and Drive:** I always keep a long-term focus. I am growing an enduring enterprise. I am driven toward the end result in all I do. I will continue to add important things to my plate. I will stop at nothing.

8. **Achieving Big Things and Solving Complex Problems:** I look to achieve very large things. I continually refine my ability to solve complex problems.

9. **Physical and Spiritual Well-Being:** I maintain healthy practices, including diet, exercise, meditation, and the avoidance of things that may damage my health.

10. **Adding Value:** I enjoy adding value wherever I can by helping things produce more and run more efficiently, from businesses to non-profits to families.

Create Your List of Deal-Breakers

Everyone needs to have a deal-breaker list. This is a list of values, behaviors, attributes, characteristics, etc., that you just won't tolerate—period. These deal-breakers can be any number of things or ideas, so let your imagination run free with this exercise. Most people find it easy to list a few deal-breakers right off the bat—you probably have no shortage of recent examples! It can take more time to distill your list down to a choice few. Again, take time with this exercise. It might help to ask yourself the following questions first:

- When was the last time you were really angry and frustrated? Why?

- What makes your life less fulfilling than you think it should be?

- What is the trait that you most deplore in others?

- What is it that you most dislike?

- What do you regard as the lowest depth of misery?

- What do you least value in your friends?

Now, on a separate document, itemize as specifically as you can your list of people or projects that cause you the most pain and grief because they don't align with your stated values. These are people and things that are holding you back, and that you must consider removing from your life. These would be things that you are letting slip past your doorman. Remember that it is far more expensive to get someone or something out of your life once they are in it, than it is to not allow them into your life or business in the first place. Think of a time in your life when you've chosen what you believe represents an opportunity over your values (we'll be going into much more detail on this in the next chapter). You'll begin to notice how this decision has cost you time, energy, and money.

The Deal-Breakers

For each of these categories below (plus any more that you'd like to add), create a list of people or projects that don't align with your values.

A. Friends and acquaintances:_____

_____

B. Partners:_____

_____

B. Projects:_____

_____

G. Business opportunities:_____

_____

C. Organizations: _____

_____

D. Colleagues/employees: _____

_____

E. Clients/vendors: _____

_____

F. Routine obligations/commitments: _____

_____

Continuing on with this exercise, create a set of rules or attributes and "anti-rules" that will help you make better decisions in your life. We've created some examples to get the creativity flowing:

Examples of rules for the people that I will let into my room from this point forward:

- They must contribute an equal amount to the relationship
- They must work in a field that has a positive impact in the world
- They must be loyal and honest
- They must be open-minded and have a sense of humor

Examples of "anti-rules" for the people that I won't let into my room from this point forward:

- I will not tolerate anyone who is controlling or narcissistic
- I will not tolerate anyone who is always late and forgetful
- I will not tolerate anyone who complains all the time and acts needy
- I will not tolerate anyone who doesn't value being fit and conscious of their health

You'll begin the process of training your doorman to prevent these impediments to your success to the extent that you can. The more conscious you are of who and what you are allowing into your life, the more you can do something about it.

Hand Your List Over to Your Doorman

This is perhaps the hardest step of all. How do you do this exactly? If your doorman is just a fictitious person in your mind who acts as a metaphor to remind you that certain people or things cannot "enter," then how does this really happen?

Easy: By carefully determining your values and applying them to your daily decision-making process, you will begin to understand the long-term implications of values-based decision making. Once you've created your list of values and your deal-breakers, you can consider your doorman officially hired. Then it's simply a matter of living up to those lists and keeping them in the forefront of your mind every single day, with every decision you make.

Chapter 25
Values-Based Decision Making

Values-Based Decision Making: Always Choose in Favor of Your Passions and Your Values

Now that you know the flow and format of these exercises, you can begin the process of adding awareness and values-based decision making to all areas of your life. Feel free to create values and rules for any category of your life. For example:

A. Projects that you are involved in

B. Charities

C. Organizations that your children are involved in

D. Your children's friends

E. Future business/career decisions

F. Your personal habits

G. Your health and well-being

H. _____

I. _____

J. _____

Journaling is an excellent way to take some time to reflect on your life and your future. Write down any ideas or thoughts that you have around this topic of values-based decision making. Would this knowledge have helped you in the past in business or key relationships? Can it help you in your parenting efforts? Will you use it to avoid mistakes? How will you create a process of re-evaluating your values when faced with a decision? What kind of practical method will you practice every time someone or something is trying to come into your life? By thinking through your values and the relationship of values to all areas of your life, you'll bring more awareness to this topic and avoid some common mistakes that move you backward instead of forward.

Once you've completed the exercises, be sure to save them in a safe place on your computer. You may also find it helpful to print them out, three-hole punch them, and keep them in a three-ring binder that you can refer to at any time.

Conclusion

In these pages, you've undertaken a partial tour of the possibilities of thinking of your life in the context of a room, where you and your own doorman manage who is in your room and what projects are there. You can say "yes," or you can say "no." While simplistic, this concept gives you the opportunity to unclutter, or to focus upon and embrace people and opportunities in a fresh way.

One of the most powerful aspects of the concept is that it is not my room. It is not someone else's room. It is *your* room. This is true for your BNI group as well as for you as an individual. You can tailor it, customize it, and use it as it best suits you. Julia Child was fond of saying that a recipe is only a starting point—some rough guidelines that you can make your own. That's how the room idea can not only be in your life, but "of" your life.

You can empower yourself to manage what you didn't think was manageable, to get back in balance, and to include whatever your life needs to make sense and be more enjoyable.

You may have detected moments of joy in the stories, as well as a sense of freedom, that can be your own. Your room and doorman can make all the difference in your life at a number of levels. Go out and use this approach, make it your own, and share it with the ones you love.

Acknowledgements

As we reviewed our conversations and work with people all over the world who are committed to the quality of the human experience, we were constantly reminded that anything worth doing takes sometimes hundreds or even thousands of courageous and gifted people to achieve successful outcomes. In the spirit of this reality we're grateful for all the talented people who have worked with us to make this book possible. Many have become good friends and are definitely in our room.

The Transformational Leadership Council and BNI communities and boards, together with Rick Sapio's network of entrepreneurs, hosted many of the conversations and workshops where this material was both presented and further developed. Many contributed stories. We thank you all for taking the time and having the courage to tell your story knowing that it may not make its way between the covers of this book.

We want to thank Ann-Marie Stillion, editorial and design consultant, David Hirning, for his wise and tasteful work as a copy editor, Douglas Silva of Midnite Graphics for the cover design and inside book layout, and Lee Gessner and his team at Franklin Green Publishing for turning our manuscript into a published book.

A special thanks to Russ Hall for his tireless work as a writing partner, our good friend Timothy Moore for nudging us to do this book, and of course Alex Mandossian for being the catalyst.

We thank our beautiful life partners—Joan Emery, Beth Misner and Melissa Sapio. Without their patience, support and love there would be no book.

With gratitude,

Stewart Emery, Ivan Misner, and Rick Sapio

—March 2014

About the Authors

Stewart Emery, Lh.D.

is co-author of the international bestsellers, *Success Built to Last and Do You Matter? How Great Design Will Make People Love Your Company.* He has a lifetime of experience as an entrepreneur, creative director, corporate consultant and executive coach. He has conducted coaching interviews with more than 12,000 people in the last four decades and is considered one of the fathers of the Human Potential Movement.

Stewart has been involved with numerous bestselling books throughout the years, including; *Actualizations: You Don't Have to Rehearse to Be Yourself* and *The Owners Manual For Your Life.* As a consultant, he asked questions that lead MasterCard to its iconic "Priceless" theme and was responsible for connecting the core team that created the Barnes & Noble *Nook* in an astonishingly brief twelve-month period.

Through leading workshops and delivering keynotes around the world, together with his books and media appearances, Stewart Emery has touched the lives of millions of people.

Ivan Misner, Ph.D.

is the Founder and Chairman of BNI, the world's largest business networking organization. BNI was founded in 1985. The organization now has thousands of chapters throughout every populated continent of the world. He serves as chairman of the board of the Referral Institute, a referral training company with trainers operating around the world.

He has written 17 books including the *New York Times* best seller *Masters of Networking* and number one bestseller *Masters of Success.*

Called the *"Father of Modern Networking"* by CNN and the *"Networking Guru"* by Entrepreneur magazine, Dr. Misner is considered to be one of the world's leading experts on business networking and has been a keynote speaker for major corporations and associations throughout the world. He has been featured in the *L.A. Times, Wall Street Journal, and New York. Times,* as well as numerous TV and radio shows including *CNN,* the *BBC* and *The Today Show on NBC.*

Rick Sapio is a life-long entrepreneur who started his first company, a bicycle repair business, after the death of his father when he was 13 years old. Since then, he has founded more than 20 companies. As the 7th of nine children, raised by a mom with serious, life-long depression issues; he learned early that it's best to think positive about the cards one's been dealt; and to carefully select who was in his room.

Rick's purpose, which is to *inspire entrepreneurship,* led him to start *A Billion Entrepreneurs*—a global movement and movie intended to inspire people to seek their life's purpose, and the freedom of entrepreneurship, regardless of their current situation.

Rick is proud of being a five-time Chairman of the "Gathering of Titans" program held at MIT in Boston. He also has a passion for teaching business, and co-founded Business Finishing School, an online program that teaches the foundational principles of business to its members.

BNI®

BNI, the world's largest business networking organization, was founded by Dr. Ivan Misner in 1985 as a way for businesspeople to generate referrals in a structured, professional environment. The organization, now the world's largest referral business network, has thousands of chapters with tens of thousands of members on every populated continent. Since its inception, BNI members have passed millions of referrals, generating billions of dollars in business for the participants.

The primary purpose of the organization is to pass qualified business referrals to its members. The philosophy of BNI may be summed up in two simple words: Givers Gain®. If you give business to people, you will get business from them. BNI allows only one person per profession to join a chapter. The program is designed to help businesspeople develop long-term relationships, thereby creating a basis for trust and, inevitably, referrals. The mission of BNI is to help members increase their business through a structured, positive, and professional word-of-mouth program that enables them to develop long-term, meaningful relationships with quality business professionals.

To visit a chapter near you, contact BNI via email at: bni@bni.com or visit www.bni.com

Notes

Notes

Notes

Notes